THE ENGLISH REFORMATION 1529–58

The English Reformation 1529–58

DAVID H. PILL M.A.

 UNIVERSITY OF LONDON PRESS LTD

ISBN 0 340 17057 3 Boards
ISBN 0 340 09416 8 Paperback

First published 1973

University of London Press Ltd
St Paul's House, Warwick Lane, London EC4P 4AH

Printed in Great Britain by
Hazell Watson & Viney Ltd, Aylesbury, Bucks

PREFACE

In view of the size, scope and aims of this book it has been necessary to rely largely on secondary authorities. Most of the books I have consulted are listed in the bibliographies, but I feel I ought to acknowledge here my special debt to the biographies of Henry VIII by Mr J. J. Bagley and Professor J. J. Scarisbrick, to Professor A. G. Dickens's justly famous history of the English Reformation, to Professor G. W. O. Woodward's account of the dissolution of the monasteries, and to Miss H. F. M. Prescott's life of Mary Tudor. I am grateful to Messrs B. T. Batsford Ltd for allowing me to quote copyright material from Professor Dickens's book, and to Messrs Methuen & Co Ltd for permission to quote from Professor G. R. Elton's *England under the Tudors*. My gratitude goes too to the staff of the Historical Association Library who have helped me obtain some of the more obscure books I have needed.

I would like to take this opportunity of thanking Dr Christopher Haigh, who painstakingly read the book in manuscript, corrected my mistakes, and made a number of very valuable suggestions, and of acknowledging the help I have received with some small points of detail from Professor C. W. Dugmore and Mr Peter Heath. Thanks are due too to Mr John O'Connell who very kindly checked the proofs. I am particularly grateful to my editor, Mr Ben Jones, for all the encouragement he has given me in the sometimes daunting task of writing my first book. Finally I wish to dedicate this work to my parents.

CONTENTS

PART 1
The English Church in 1529

[1] ITS MEMBERS

The Pope

In 1529, when Englishmen went to Mass in their parish church they heard the celebrant pray for Clement their Pope. Clement was an Italian prince, a member of the famous Medici family, ruler of a vast area of central Italy, and, caught up as he was in the great struggle between the royal houses of France and Spain being fought out on the Italian peninsula, of necessity a politician. But he was also the Bishop of Rome, the successor of Peter, prince of the Apostles, and as such the Vicar of Christ, the spiritual head of western Christendom. That body was united by loyalty to him, by adherence to a set of international laws, existing side by side with the law of kings and parliaments, and laid down in the massive and unwieldy *Corpus Juris Canonici*, and by a common Faith, strengthened by seven divinely ordained sacraments.

Englishmen were not only bound to pray for their Pope, but to pay taxes for his support. One was an annual payment called Peter's Pence. Originally it had been a tax of a penny on every hearth, but by the twelfth century it had been fixed at £199·33, and the Popes had never got any more and sometimes got a great deal less. The English bishops, however, were required to hand over to them a proportion of the income from their see in their first year of office in the form of a tax called Annates, as a thank-offering for their appointment. Then, in theory at least, all beneficed clergymen were annually liable to pay the Pope a tenth of what had been the spiritual income (that is the tithes and offerings) of their living in 1292, but not all of this money got to Rome, for there were many exemptions and the tax collectors themselves took a sizeable share.

The Pope had the power to grant, in exchange for money, certain privileges and dispensations, including the right of a clergyman to hold livings in plurality, and, at a price, appeals could be made against decisions in the English Church courts to the Holy See, though cases which could be tried in the King's courts had been forbidden hearings abroad by the Statute of *Praemunire* of 1393.

The bishops of the two English provinces of Canterbury and York needed papal edicts called bulls confirming their election before they could take up their office, and no archbishop could exercise his jurisdiction until he had petitioned for and been granted the *pallium*, a vestment which symbolized a sharing in the Pope's authority and could cost £1,000.

It is easy, however, to exaggerate both the amount of money going to Rome and the power its bishop had in England. Even in 1529, final authority in this country belonged to its King, who took far more from the English Church than the Pope did. His permission had to be sought before papal bulls could be published in his kingdom; despite the international nature of the Church, foreigners could not hold benefices here without his licence, and those who had it had to pay a double amount of tax; he had the right to appoint to a large number of livings, a right with which the fourteenth-century statute of Provisors forbade the Pope to interfere; and he decided which clerics should be elected bishops, and was therefore sure of their loyalty. Even the Pope's special representative in England, his Legate *a latere*, Thomas Wolsey, was King Henry's servant, not his.

The bishops

There were in England and Wales two archbishops, of Canterbury and York, and nineteen diocesan bishops. In general they were men of quite humble origin but of academic distinction and administrative ability, who were useful to the King and had earned preferment by loyal service which they continued to give when entrusted with a diocese. Thus Wolsey was, among other things, Lord Chancellor; Cuthbert Tunstall, Bishop of London, was Keeper of the Privy Seal; and John Veysey, Bishop of Exeter, was President of the Council of Wales. Other bishops (and most of them were civil lawyers by training, and not theologians) served the King on embassies abroad or on commissions at home, and all of them were members of the House of Lords. The Bishop of Worcester, Jerome Ghinucci, was an Italian who worked in Henry's interests at the papal court, and another Italian, Lorenzo Campeggio, was Bishop of Salisbury.

Although the bishops, as the King's servants or as non-resident foreigners, were often unable to officiate in their dioceses, their duties there, pastoral and administrative, were still carried out – by deputy. Such tasks as could only be performed by men in episcopal orders, such as ordaining, confirming, and consecrating churches and altars, were generally passed on to bishops *in partibus infidelium*, titular heads of dioceses in areas under heathen rule, who were usually abbots or priors of English monasteries. Other suffragan bishops had Irish dioceses, but preferred England to that wild country. Such men were not given a regular wage for their work as suffragans, but received fees for performing particular tasks. In addition they were given well-endowed parishes, where they did not carry out their duties as parish priests, but nevertheless received the normal stipend. And so the scandal of non-residence spread downwards.

The day-to-day administration of a diocese was in the hands of the vicar-general. He was usually a university graduate with some training in civil or canon law, who, like the suffragan, had a good income from a number of rich parishes. It was on his orders that the suffragans carried out their tasks, and it was he who instituted priests to new livings (that is, committed to them the spiritual care of their parishioners). He granted licences to seek ordination outside the diocese, where more convenient, to ordinands; to preach and to say Mass, to unbeneficed clergy; and to absent themselves from their parishes in order to study or go on pilgrimage, to the beneficed. The vicar-general had some degree of responsibility for the maintenance of the parish churches of the diocese and of their chapels of ease. He ordered enquiries into defects in church buildings and furnishings, and into cases of suspected bloodshed in churchyards, a circumstance which necessitated an act of reconsecration. Among the other miscellaneous duties he had was that of giving people the right to collect money for such things as the building of bridges and lighthouses, the repair of city walls and the maintenance of leper hospitals, and to give indulgences in exchange (see below, p. 38). The vicar-general also granted permission for couples to marry within the prohibited degrees of relationship and without the banns being called thrice as prescribed. A record of each of his official acts was entered in the general diocesan register by the bishop's registrar who also kept a record of ordinations. It is from documents such as these that historians have gained their knowledge of the workings of the medieval Church.

When the bishop was in his diocese, the vicar-general's authority usually lapsed, and some of the bishops, if absent at other times, are known to have carried out triennial visitations of their dioceses, when they checked that the clergy were doing their duty, and collected procurations, or fees in lieu of entertainment, from the parishes or monasteries visited.

Each diocese had a bishop's palace in the cathedral city and was usually well provided with episcopal manors (the Bishop of Wells had twenty-four) where the bishop could stay as he made his visitation. It was the land attached to these residences which brought in the bulk of the episcopal income. There was little to be gained, particularly by a non-resident, from the other (spiritual) sources of income which included fees for institutions and for the blessing of newly elected abbots and priors, the fruits of vacant livings, and synodals – that is dues of usually not more than two shillings a year paid by the incumbent of each parish as tribute to his bishop. However, with its manors, palace, and town house in London, a bishopric was a welcome reward for a royal servant. Wolsey's old bishopric of Lincoln, for instance, was worth over £2,000 a year in 1535, but there were others like St Asaph, valued at £131 11s 6d, which brought in considerably less.

Another source of episcopal revenue were the fees paid in the diocesan courts. In some dioceses – Exeter for example – there were two courts of which the bishop was theoretically the chief judge – the court of audience and the consistory. Others, such as Coventry and Lichfield, had only the consistory. The functions of the Court of Audience, which the bishop sometimes presided over in his own house, differed from diocese to diocese. However, it was probably chiefly concerned with appeals from lower courts or with cases arising from trouble discovered on visitation.

The presidency of the consistory court was usually delegated to an officer called the official-principal. The court had jurisdiction over cases which involved breaches of the canon law by clergy or laity. These included heresy, fornication, matrimonial and testamentary disputes, the non-payment of fees due to the Church, perjury, defamation and assaults on clergymen. The parties involved in a case did not usually plead their suits themselves; they nominated counsel called proctors to do it for them. In some cases, called *ex-officio*, often brought by informers, the court itself prosecuted, and the accused was made to take an oath to tell the truth which it would have been perjury to break.

The primary sanction imposed by the court on a defendant, often as a result of non-appearance in court, was, in the case of a layman, suspension from attending church, and in the case of a clergyman, suspension from celebrating the sacraments. When a suspended person was particularly stubborn and suspension was of no effect, he would be liable to excommunication. Being excommunicate he would not be allowed to sit on a jury or be a witness in court, he would be unable to sue for the recovery of lands or debt, and his will would not be proved. Excommunication and suspension could be disposed of if absolution were sought in the court. Before the judge would grant it, the accused would have to pay the fee due to the court's registrar for the letters of suspension and excommunication which had been sent to his parish priest to notify him of the sentences. In a case of continued disobedience, even after excommunication, the court could apply to the Court of Chancery for a writ *de excommunicato capiendo*, and it would then be the secular authority's task to arrest the offender and commit him to prison.

Another writ, *de heretico comburendo*, was applied for when a defendant was found guilty of that most serious offence against religion, heresy, so that the sinner could be burnt. However, usually the worst punishment a man found guilty of an offence by a church court had to face was a penance. He would perhaps be required to walk round his parish church before the processional cross, barefoot with a candle in his hand, though often penances were commuted to fines. Appeal could be made against the decision of a consistory court in the province of Canterbury to the Court of Arches, while in the province of York appeals might go to the Archbishop's Court of Chancery. From these courts there was, in theory at least, right of appeal to Rome.

The Archbishop of Canterbury traditionally had legatine authority, that is local use of the powers of the Holy See (an authority still represented in his right to grant degrees), and Archbishop Warham stretched it to make appeals to Rome well-nigh impossible. However, his authority as *legatus natus* came to be overshadowed by Wolsey's powers as *legatus a latere*. Indeed, Wolsey is said to have established his legatine court at Westminster in an attempt to supersede all existing ecclesiastical courts. Both archbishops had supervisory rights over the bishops in their provinces and could hold visitations of the dioceses, during the course of which the diocesan bishops' rights were suspended. When a man died owning goods worth over £10 in more than one diocese, probate had to take place in the archbishop's Prerogative Court. The archbishop presided over the Convocation of his province, a sort of clerical parliament which could make laws for the Church and grant taxes to the King. It was attended by the bishops, abbots and priors of the province, deans of cathedrals and collegiate churches, archdeacons, and proctors representing cathedral, collegiate and parish clergy.

The archdeacons

In each diocese there was at least one archdeaconry; larger dioceses were divided into several. The archdeacon had general supervisory powers in his area, which he exercised through visitation, and he was sometimes referred to as *oculus episcopi*. As his title implies, he originally had particular authority over all deacons and persons in lower orders; he had been responsible not only for their conduct, but also their instruction, and it was he who had presented them to the bishop for ordination. Now, in person or by deputy, he inducted newly instituted clergy, that is put them into possession of the temporalities of their parishes, and similarly admitted churchwardens into their office.

By the sixteenth century, archdeacons generally seem to have been neglecting their duties. Their work was often done by deputy, and in some cases archdeaconries were farmed out for a term of years to people who were entitled to collect procurations and other fees due to the archdeacon.

The archdeacon usually had the right to hold a court, but it did not always function, and when it did was generally presided over by a person known as the archdeacon's official. The cases over which it had jurisdiction varied from diocese to diocese. In some dioceses it might deal with many of the matters which the consistory dealt with in others; in other areas its jurisdiction was confined to the proving of wills.

Certain areas in an archdeaconry were outside the archdeacon's jurisdiction. These districts, known as peculiars, were under the jurisdiction of the owners of the local manors or churches. These might be particular monasteries, whole orders (for example the Gilbertines and the Premonstratensians, who were exempt from diocesan jurisdiction), the King, the archbishop, the local bishop or one from another see, or the dean and chapter of the cathedral.

Once many of what were nominally the archdeacon's functions in the sixteenth century had been carried out by rural deans. Dioceses were still divided into deaneries, but while in some dioceses such as York and Lichfield their deans retained considerable testamentary powers, they had in many places ceased to have any jurisdiction. They might, however, occasionally be delegated such a duty as looking after a parish during an inter-regnum by the diocesan authorities.

The cathedral clergy

The archdeacon was often a member of the chapter or governing body of the cathedral, the bishop's church, where he had his *cathedra* or throne. The chapter, so called because of the way the daily meeting of the brethren in a monastery began with the reading of a chapter of the Rule of the order, was originally the *familia* or household of the bishop; now it was largely independent of his authority.

There were two types of cathedral, monastic and secular. There were eight monastic cathedrals, that is Canterbury, Carlisle, Durham, Ely, Norwich, Rochester, Winchester and Worcester, of which all but Carlisle, a house of Augustinian canons, were in the custody of the Benedictine order. In the monastic cathedrals the chapter consisted of the prior and convent, and the high officials were appointed by the prior. The bishop was the honorary abbot, and occupied the abbot's stall in choir. We shall, however, be looking at the monasteries more closely later, so we will confine our interest to the secular cathedrals here.

There were nine secular cathedrals in England, that is Chichester, Exeter, Hereford, Lichfield, Lincoln, Salisbury, Wells and York, though in the dioceses of Lichfield and Wells respectively, monastic churches at Conventry and Bath also contained bishops' thrones. All four Welsh cathedrals were secular. Membership of a secular chapter was an honour conferred by the bishop on a successful clergyman and usually led to a considerable increase in the income of the member, or canon, as he was called. His prebend or stipend either took the form of a sum of money or, more commonly, of the revenues of a church or manor, or both, attached to a particular canonry. The ownership of a prebend based on a parish church did not necessarily mean a canon had to serve that church as its priest, since deputies were not hard to find: nor did he always have to reside at the cathedral, for the place of non-residents in the choir was supplied by vicars-choral. Each canon had one, and together they formed a corporate body, a second collegiate foundation in the church. There were usually chantry priests too, and at York Minster the total staff of clergy was well over a hundred. Such large bodies must have been difficult to supervise, but such was the responsibility of the cathedral dignitaries. The dean was the elected chairman of the chapter, occupying that position with respect to it which had originally been held by the bishop. He had responsibility for the spiritual welfare of all those living in the cathedral precincts, and archidiaconal authority over the cathedral city and churches attached to prebends. The precentor was in charge of all persons and things connected with divine service; the treasurer was the guardian of the fabric, furniture and ornaments of the church; and the chancellor was secretary of the chapter and had charge of the cathedral school and library and responsibility for seeing that sermons were regularly preached. It was the chapter who in theory chose the bishop but in fact they merely elected the King's nominee, when they received his *congé d'élire* or leave to elect.

The parish clergy

There were upwards of 9,000 parishes in England and each in theory had a priest whose responsibility it was to offer Christ again for the sins of the world in the Holy Sacrifice of the Mass and to say the divine offices (or daily services), to baptize his flock, to prepare them for confirmation, to hear their confessions and absolve them, to give them Holy Communion, to preach to them at least four times a year, to visit them on their sick bed and anoint them with the oil of Holy Unction, and to bury them.

To be a priest a man had in theory to be twenty-four years old, morally suitable and of a certain educational standard, and have some means of livelihood. He should also have received the first tonsure and been admitted to the minor orders of ostiary (door keeper), lector, exorcist and acolyte (candle bearer), and to the sacred orders of subdeacon and deacon. The subdeacon was one of the three ministers at High Mass, where he prepared the bread and wine and the vessels, and read the Epistle. A deacon could read the Gospel at the same service and had the right to baptize, but only a person admitted to priest's orders could celebrate Mass.

It has been estimated that there was one cleric for every fifty laymen, and it sometimes happened that a hundred or more men were priested at a time, so some doubt has been expressed as to the thoroughness with which ordination candidates were examined. There were certainly wide variations in the standard of education reached by ordinands. In the bishops' registers, men presented to livings are usually described as either *magistri* (that is Masters of Arts) or *domini*, and the latter generally far outnumber the former. In the diocese of Lincoln for instance, between 1495 and 1520, 1,168 *domini* were appointed to livings, but only 261 *magistri*. The word *dominus* can in this case mean any number of things. Some of the men so described might have been Bachelors of Arts, while others might once have been pupils at one or other of the many new grammar schools founded at the end of the fifteenth and beginning of the sixteenth century and have learnt some Latin. Others might only have attended petty or A.B.C. schools where there was no Latin teaching but where they would have learnt to read their native tongue. They would then have been able to improve their learning by reading some of the ever increasing number of printed books. Mrs Bowker, to whose researches we owe the Lincoln figures, thinks that the standard of education among clergy was probably higher than ever, though few of them received any specifically theological training. In 1529, however, the convocation of Canterbury did order priests to spend two or three hours, at least three days a week, in approved devotional reading. But many of them never read the Bible, for the authorized version was in Latin, a language they could not understand and, incidentally, the language they had to say Mass in.

Candidates for ordination were required to have a 'title' or guaranteed living of not less than five marks a year (a mark was 67p). Most ordinands, who generally came from humble peasant families, were granted titles by monasteries. Of 795 men raised to the priesthood in the diocese of Exeter between 1519 and 1539, 540 served monastic titles and only three were ordained to their own patrimony – that is had some private means of support. The rest were given titles by colleges or by the dean and chapter of the cathedral, though a lucky half-dozen had livings to go to. 110 of the candidates were monks or friars; it is possible that the 430 secular ordinands given titles by the monasteries served as chaplains to the parish churches which they controlled or per-haps served the altars of chantry foundations of which they were trustees, though it may be that their 'titles' were purely nominal.

Most newly ordained priests probably spent a few years as stipendiary curates, assisting or taking the place of an incumbent, or as chantry chaplains saying Mass for the souls of the founders of their chantries, while others would serve as domestic chaplains in the houses of country gentlemen and noblemen. In the North, where parishes were often six to ten times the size of southern parishes, there were comparatively few opportunities for pro-motion to a benefice and the majority of the clergy spent the whole of their working lives in such capacities. To get a parish, a priest had first to find a patron, for the advowson, or right to present to a living, was generally owned by an individual or corporation, perhaps the descendant or successors of the foun-ders of the church. When he had found one he would again be examined as to his education and morals and then instituted and inducted, or, where the bishop was patron, simply collated to his living. He would then have the title of rector or vicar. Both these names have very precise meanings, though today the latter is being increasingly used very loosely to describe any Protestant minister. Once there were only rectors. They had sole charge of a parish and in payment for the work they did were given the full tithes or tenths of the agricultural produce of the parish together with an area of land called glebe, which they farmed themselves. In the eleventh and twelfth centuries, however, parochial benefices had frequently been given to monasteries as part of their endownment, in the belief that the monks would make better provision for the spiritual wants of the people than had been made before, and would spend their surplus revenues in works of piety and charity. In time, however, many monasteries failed to make proper provision for the care and instruction of the people, sometimes employing some poor, inadequately paid clergyman as their deputy or vicar to perform the necessary services. The Lateran Council of 1215 therefore decreed that all appropriators of benefices should provide perpetual vicars, and church and parliamentary laws made in England insisted on the regular endowment of vicarages. Often it was arranged that the appropriators should take the great tithes of corn, hay and wood, and that the vicar should have the rectory or another suitable house to live in, the glebe, small tithes of wool, dairy produce, livestock, and, in theory at least, of the profits of labour and trade, and offerings. But there were in fact variations in the way vicarages were endowed and some monasteries allotted their vicars stipends after they had received all the tithes and offerings themselves. Appropriations still went on and there were still some parishes which did not have vicars but were served by members of the proprietary body or by curates appointed by them and, unlike the vicars, removable at will. Rectories were not necessarily more valuable than vicarages. The income of the incumbent usually depended on the size of the parish, some rectories being worth less than £5 a year and some vicarages £50. Even where a rectory was valuable, the rector's expenses were often considerable, since he was responsible for all procurations, and had to keep the rectory house and the chancel of the church in good repair (a duty not incumbent on a vicar). Then sometimes he had to pay a curate or find a pension for a previous occupant of the living, usually about a third of its gross value. Mr Peter Heath has suggested that an income of at least £15 a year was necessary for an incumbent to be able to defray his expenses and enjoy a reasonable standard of living if he employed a curate, and £10 if he did not, but his own researches have led him to believe that probably three-quarters of all the parochial livings in

England were worth less than £15, and half of them less than £10.

Where a rector or vicar was non-resident, all his pastoral work might be done by a stipendiary curate. In some parishes the church contained a number of chantry chapels and their priests too could be required to assist the parish priest or deputize for him. Other parish churches, like that of Manchester for instance, had a collegiate organization, perhaps being staffed by three or more clergymen living in community, but membership of such a college was by this time often a sinecure.

The laity

In 1497 the Venetian ambassador Andrea Trevisan wrote of the English,

... they all attend Mass everyday, and say many Paternosters in public ... they always hear Mass on Sunday in their parish church, and give liberal alms ... nor do they omit any form incumbent on good Christians.

Indeed pre-Reformation England was noted for its devotion to the Faith and for the richness of the ornaments of its churches. To quote Trevisan again,

... above all their riches are displayed in the church treasures; for there is not a parish church in the kingdom so mean as not to possess crucifixes, candlesticks, censers, patens and cups of silver.

This picture, which is probably equally true of the Church in England in 1529, was probably based on observation of life in the towns, but churchwardens' accounts reveal that even remote country churches were lovingly cared for by parishioners for whom the parish church was the very centre of life. The church-wardens were the people responsible for the administration of church money and property. They were laymen (or women) and usually two in number, one being chosen by the parish priest and the other by the people, and were responsible for the main-tenance of the nave and for rendering the annual account of income and expenditure. A good deal of a church's income came from parish property. One town church received rents from ten

tenements, and at a country church special wardens were appointed for the care of lambs, sheep and hogs, while there was a
swarm of bees to provide wax for altar candles. In some parishes
there were wardens for each altar or shrine who rendered their
own account at the annual parish meeting. They received gifts
of clothing which they sold, perhaps in the medieval equivalent
of a jumble sale, to make money for purposes specified by the
donor, such as the purchase of a saint's statue or a new cope.
Money was also made by letting out the church house, a sort of
medieval parish hall. In the parish accounts of Stratton in
Cornwall several references are made to the occupancy of the
church house by gypsies, and in 1526 the 'keepers of the bear'
paid 1p rent for it. Other methods of raising money were by
letting out vestments and plate to other, less fortunate churches
for funerals and festivals, and by selling seats in church, though
the appropriation of seats had long been frowned upon by the
ecclesiastical authorities. Sometimes, of course, the parish church
would receive bequests in parishioners' wills, and sometimes
general levies were made on the whole parish. In one Devon
parish every parishioner of independent means had to pay a
penny a year in wax silver to provide a light to burn before the
Holy Rood, the great crucifix which stood on the chancel screen,
and their hired servants had to pay a halfpenny. A more popular
way of raising money was by the sale of church ales brewed in
the church house.

The wardens were expected to carry out other parochial duties
unconnected with the maintenance of the church, such as
collecting Peter's Pence or levying a rate for the maintenance of
a bridge. They were also supposed to report on the condition
of the church fabric and the behaviour of their priest when
visitations were made. Their job was not always a popular one
and sometimes those elected refused it and were fined or taken
before the consistory court for doing so.

In some parishes there was a church council of three, four or
more men who received surplus revenue from the wardens of the
shrines for the general benefit of the church and were involved in
general administration within, and church business without the

parish. Next in importance to them and the churchwaı
the parish clerk. He was sometimes known as the *aquaebo*
because he was responsible for the provision of holy wate
in the rites of the Church. Today he might be called the sexton,
the verger or simply the caretaker. He was expected to help the
priest sing some of the services, and was responsible for the
general maintenance of the church. Besides the wardens and the
clerk, a church might be served by bellringers and an organist.

The parish of the early sixteenth century was self-sufficient.
Not only did the community as a whole contribute towards the
maintenance of their part of the church, the nave, and also towards civil costs in the parish, they paid the incumbent the
greater part, sometimes the whole of his income. They did this
through tithes and payments for the reading of the bede-roll,
a list of dead parishioners for whom prayers were asked, and for
obits, memorial services on the anniversaries of parishioners'
deaths. Sometimes too they made a contribution towards the
upkeep of the rector's chancel, often by far the most dilapidated
part of a church.

To all appearances then the English were a charitable, church-
going people, devout to the point of superstition, spending a lot
of their time reading (if they could read, that is) devotional
literature, going on pilgrimage to shrines like those of St Thomas
at Canterbury, St Chad at Lichfield, and St Cuthbert at Durham,
and joining guilds, not necessarily craft guilds, but mutual benefit societies which provided members with splendid funerals and
obits and usually had some charitable intent towards the
Church. Chantries were still being endowed and new churches
built. There is much left to remind us of early sixteenth-century
devotion – Henry VII's Chapel in Westminster Abbey, St
George's Chapel at Windsor, the fine parish churches at Laven-
ham in Suffolk, and Launceston in Cornwall, and a great deal
else besides. An age of faith indeed, but let us mark some more
of the words of the Venetian ambassador, words even more
appropriate in 1529 than when he wrote them thirty years before:
... there are, however, many who have various opinions concerning
religion.

[2] ITS PROBLEMS

Anti-clericalism

There has always been a tendency among churchgoers to be hypocritical, to expect their pastor to adhere to a stricter code of Christian living than they are willing to adhere to themselves. In the early sixteenth century, when the standard required of a priest was clearly expressed in canon law and when almost every parishioner took an interest in the affairs of his parish church, people were more ready than now to take their criticism of their parish priest to the ears of the ecclesiastical authorities. Clergymen were reported at visitations for such crimes as not keeping the chancel in good repair, not preaching or wearing a surplice, not holding processions, not visiting the sick, celebrating Mass only once a week and at inconvenient times, letting their hair grow too long and wearing unsuitable clothes, spending too much time in the inn, and playing football.

Perhaps we should not attach too much significance to the reports made to episcopal and archidiaconal visitors by church-wardens who were sworn to declare any faults in their parishes, but there is little doubt that there was considerable anti-clericalism among certain sections of the population. It was no new phenomenon, but it gained strength, particularly among the middle class, as, partly as a result of the expansion of grammar school education, the laity became increasingly literate. There was little criticism where there was little education.

Merchants disagreed with the Church's teaching against usury, while townsmen's hostility to the ecclesiastical authorities had been increased by long struggles by town councils against cathedrals and monasteries with rival powers. Men objected to being spied upon and dragged before an ecclesiastical court for some slight moral lapse; they objected also to clergymen guilty of capital crimes escaping the death penalty by claiming the right to be judged in the Church's courts instead of the King's. It was said that criminals deliberately took minor orders merely to enable them to claim what was known as benefit of clergy, and therefore get a lesser sentence than they would have got in the secular court. In 1512 Parliament had enacted, temporarily, that murderers and robbers in minor orders should be subject to the secular law, and Wolsey had since obtained a bull from Pope Clement to allow one bishop and two abbots or dignitaries to degrade a clerk. This made the problem easier to deal with, but it should be noted that anyone able to read the first verse of the fifty-first psalm (the 'Neck Verse') was entitled to trial in a Church court, it having long ago been assumed that only someone in clerical orders would be literate. However, it had recently been decided that a layman should only be allowed to 'plead his clergy' once.

Among other things which were resented were the monetary exactions of a rich Church which owned a fifth of the land in England, land which many laymen coveted. Men bridled not only at having to pay their tithe and Peter's Pence, but also at having to produce mortuary dues and probate fees, charges from which the very poor were normally exempt. A mortuary was usually equal in value to a deceased person's best beast or item of clothing and was a death duty due to the church in which he had received the Sacrament. It could only be pardoned when the deceased had so little property that by giving one of his animals to the Church and another to his lord his family would be left with nothing, and some clergy were unwilling to exempt anyone from mortuary charges. An extreme example of a dispute over mortuaries is the Hunne case. In 1511 Richard Hunne, a London merchant tailor, was asked by a priest for the sheet in which his dead baby was carried to the grave. Hunne refused to pay this mortuary on the ground that the sheet had not been the child's property. The priest took him to court, but Hunne's reaction was to accuse the cleric of breaking the *praemunire* law by doing so. After a long series of lawsuits over the matter, Hunne was found hanged in the Bishop's prison. Although there was much more to the case than mortuary and *praemunire*, including a charge of heresy against Hunne and a plea by the diocesan authorities that he had hanged himself, it was believed that he had been murdered for suing a *praemunire*. There was a passionate outburst of anti-clericalism in London and, after a coroner's jury had accused the Bishop's chancellor and two of his servants of murder, an important debate about the powers lay courts had over the clergy, presided over by the King himself. We shall look at the proceedings of that debate more closely later.

There were many cases brought before the ecclesiastical courts about the non-payment of tithe, and one of the reasons for this may be that the tithes collected were not always put to their proper use. Some of the tithe should have been used by the rector who received it for the maintenance of the chancel of his church, but many chancels were in a state of decay. Then it was the duty of the Church to take care of the poor, and monastic proprietors of livings were supposed to set aside some portion of tithe (usually a third) for the relief of their poorer parishioners, but this duty was frequently neglected and sometimes bishops felt bound to sequestrate the fruits of livings to distribute them among the poor. Some religious houses took the tithe and did not even make sure there was a priest available to look after the spiritual wellbeing of their parishioners.

Some clergy neglected their parishes because they were away studying, or on pilgrimage, or had other duties to perform in the service of King or bishop, some of them even letting out the right to collect tithe to laymen. The King's and bishops' servants usually held the richest livings, given them in payment for their services, and often they held them in plurality. A clergyman who wished to hold three or more livings was able to apply to the Pope for a licence to do so, but to hold two no such licence was required. Sometimes the pluralists were not even priests and would therefore have been unable to exercise the incumbent's office had they resided in their parishes. Thomas Linacre, King Henry's physician, was Rector of Holsworthy, Devon and of Wigan, Lancashire (the richest parish in England), Canon of St Stephen's Chapel, Westminster and Precentor of York Minster when he was a mere deacon. Reginald Pole, who became dean of the collegiate church at Wimborne in Dorset at the age of

eighteen, was not even a deacon when he became Dean of Exeter
nine years later; in fact he was not admitted to that order until
he became a cardinal at thirty-eight, but he performed useful
service for the King in France! His predecessor at Exeter,
Richard Pace, His Majesty's ambassador to Venice, had held the
deanery there together with those of St Paul's and Salisbury,
the archdeaconry of Dorset, four prebends, two rectories and
two vicarages, as well as the readership in Greek at Cambridge.
It was the university graduate who was most likely to be the
pluralist, for his talents were highly valued outside the parochial
sphere. The best priests were perhaps those without a degree and
with only one benefice which they were forced to stay in, but
with an increasingly literate laity (and Sir Thomas More estimated that more than half the men in England could read) they
were very much open to criticism on grounds of ignorance.

Sometimes livings were filled with people with no other quali-
fication than kinship with the patron. Some were held by members of the same family for generations. Thomas Wolsey, who,
as Archbishop of York, Bishop of Winchester, and administrator
of the sees of Worcester and Salisbury, was the only bishop with
a plurality of dioceses, made careful provision for the future of
his son Thomas Wynter. He was Dean of Wells while he was still
a schoolboy, and, as the years went by, further preferments were
provided until his income from the Church came to £2,700 a year.
His father kept most of this, though, making him an annual
allowance of £200. Wolsey, the would-be reformer of the Church,
gave, in his own conduct, one of the worst examples of its abuses.
The ideals of apostolic poverty and Christian humility were quite
alien to his nature. He acted like a king and expected to be treated
like one, and yet he could denounce the pride of the clergy. Legate
and Chancellor, he ruled the English Church as he ruled the
English people, overriding the traditional liberties of both,
incurring the hatred of both clergy and laity, and increasing
the bitterness of educated laymen against clerical power.

Not only did Wolsey have a son, but he had a daughter too
whom he placed as a nun in Shaftesbury Abbey. Secular clergy,
though they took no vow of chastity, were forbidden to marry by

canon law, but clerical incontinence, while perhaps not as com-
monplace as some would like to think, was by no means unknown.
Of the incumbents of 1,006 parishes in the Lincoln diocese
inspected in episcopal visitations between 1514 and 1521, 126
had women living with them. Priests often needed housekeepers,
and in 24 cases an immoral relationship was not suspected.
In 18 cases such a relationship was definitely suspected, and in 7
immorality was proved. In the other 77 cases the visitation
records do not make it clear whether the relationship was suspect
or not. It would be wrong to think that all the guilty priests
were promiscuous. It is likely that most of them would have
married their mistresses if they had been allowed to, and that,
as it was, they remained faithful to them. However, they were
not allowed to marry and their parishioners were not slow to
complain about their behaviour at visitation time. Critics of the
Church who took advantage of the growing popularity of the
printed word used clerical incontinence as one of their chief
weapons against it. One of the most scurrilous of these, the
London lawyer Simon Fish, a member of a group with a professional jealousy of the church courts and a desire for State to
triumph over Church, wrote, in his *Supplication for Beggars*,
addressed to the King:

Yea, and what do they more? Truly nothing but apply themselves,
by all the sleights they may, to have to do with every man's wife,
every man's daughter, and every man's maid, that cuckoldry and
bawdry should reign over all among your subjects, that no man should
know his own child.

That is one view of the clergy, but Sir Thomas More in his
Dialogue gives us another:

I boldly say that the spiritualty of England, and especially that part
in which we most find fault, that is to wit that part which we commonly call the secular clergy, is in learning and honest living well
able to match number for number the spiritualty of any nation
Christian.

There is much in what More says. The Church in England was
probably less corrupt than anywhere else in Europe with the

possible exception of Spain, and certainly was less so than in the Pope's Italy. Gross scandals among the hierarchy were by comparison unknown. Even if most bishops spent their time in the King's service and lived in splendour, their lives were generally blameless, and there were a few who, like John Fisher of Rochester, lived the lives of scholarly saints, or who diligently carried out their pastoral duties. Where the bishops did not reside, their sacred ministry was adequately performed by suffragan and, although there were many pluralists and non-residents, so large was the body of clergy that it was always possible for a vicar-general to call on some chantry or stripendiary priest to serve a parish in the place of its rector. Though there were priests who lived in sin, there were many who did not; and while there were many priests who were complained of at visitation (and generally their crimes were pretty petty) there must have been plenty who, even in that anti-clerical age, were loved by their parishioners as their faithful pastors, the inspiration of their own manifest devotion.

Lollardy

Englishmen might criticize their clergy and resent the jurisdiction of the church courts and clerical exactions, but the great mass of them held fast to the Faith taught to them by their priests, received the Sacrament and carried out their religious duties. There were some, however, who disagreed with much that was fundamental to the organization of the Church, and held their own prayer meetings, looking for a return to the ideal of apostolic poverty and true Christian living. They were called Lollards, though no one really knows why. Some say it is a name derived from the old Dutch verb *lollen*, meaning to mumble, a reference to their prayers or their preaching.

Though some scholars have felt that Lollardy had its roots in the Waldensian and other continental hersies of the thirteenth and fourteenth centuries, it is generally regarded as being of native growth and John Wycliffe is considered to have been its inspiration. Wycliffe was a famous Oxford scholar who attracted the favourable notice of Edward III's son, John of Gaunt, and was, in 1374, presented to the Crown living of Lutterworth. At that time the Pope was living in Avignon and was thought to be under the domination of England's enemy the King of France. Parliament was involved in an attack on papal power, particularly on the Pope's claim to be able to present men to English livings, and Wycliffe was called upon to give them his professional advice. He took a strong anti-papal line, asserting that the King was God's vice-regent and had the power and duty to deprive unworthy churchmen of their positions. Pope Gregory XI sent bulls ordering his arrest but his powerful patronage prevented this. In 1377 there occurred a Great Schism in the Church, with rival Popes at Rome and Avignon. Now Wycliffe came out in open opposition not just to the abuses of the Papacy but to the office itself. Regarding the Bible as the true source of authority rather than the Pope, he argued that all men should read and study it. In 1380–4 the Bible was indeed translated into English, but whether Wycliffe had a part in this work is by no means certain.

Wycliffe's own reading of the Scriptures caused him to doubt the doctrine of transubstantiation, the belief that the bread and wine consecrated in the Mass becomes the actual Body and Blood of Jesus. He substituted for it something akin to what became known as consubstantiation. He wrote,

Christ is at once God and Man, so the Sacrament is at once the Body of Christ and bread – bread and wine naturally, the Body and Blood sacramentally.

At this he lost the support of John of Gaunt but was protected from the ecclesiastical authorities by his University of Oxford and was able to die peacefully in 1384.

Those who took it upon themselves to promulgate Wycliffe's doctrines, however, were persecuted. Giving the laity the Bible to read they showed them that there was the ultimate truth and there was no need for a priest to act as intermediary between them and God; but the Church regarded itself as the guardian of the truth and was unwilling to share the task with laymen, so it did all that was possible to root out the heresy and destroy the Bible. It had an ally in a new King, Henry IV, a usurper who felt he needed its support to keep his throne. A law was passed which said that all heretics were to be burnt, and the King and Archbishop Arundel suppressed what was left of Wycliffe's heresy in the University where it had been born and nurtured. From that time few scholars adhered to the movement, though it had many adherents among the country gentry, and the King did not feel strong enough to prevent the knights of the shire in Parliament from petitioning for the disendowment of the Church. The next King, Henry V, made it clear on his accession, however, that he would resolutely support the bishops in suppressing Lollardy. This led to a rising under Sir John Oldcastle but it was promptly crushed and Lollardy was deserted by the knights and many of the merchants, who not only feared for their lives and possessions, but were alienated from the movement by the political and social radicalism of many of its adherents.

There were still many Lollards, however, among craftsmen, artisans, rural peasants and poor priests. They met in secret, and passages from the Bible or some Lollard work such as *The Lantern of Life* or *The Wycket* were read. In the latter was a very radical interpretation of a sacrament as 'but a sign or mind of a thing past', and this seems to have been the interpretation generally placed by Lollards on the Sacrament of the Altar. In the late 1420s the gaols were full of heretics awaiting trial, and in 1431 the government was alarmed by a conspiracy to confiscate the lands of the Church and use them for the maintenance of the poor and more parish priests. Bishop Reginald Pecock was so disturbed by the growth in the number of Lollards in the middle decades of the century that he wrote many books to convert them, believing persuasion to be a better way of dealing with them than burning.

Then the Lollards seem to have faded from the limelight. Perhaps civil war distracted the authorities' attention away from them. They continued to meet in secret, keeping very much to themselves and marrying only within the sect, their peace broken by the occasional raid when the local bishop was an

avowed opponent of heresy. They had their strongholds in the
villages of the Chiltern Hills, the little cloth towns on the Essex–
Suffolk border, the villages of West Kent and East Sussex, and
in scattered communities along the Thames valley and in Berk-
shire, Wiltshire and the Cotswolds. They had their adherents
too among the merchants of London, Bristol and other southern
ports, and occasionally a book expressing Lollard doctrines crops
up in the will of an East Anglian priest. There were raids on
Lollard cells in villages in Kent in 1511, in Buckinghamshire
villages in 1521, and the Essex towns and London in 1528.
In 1511–12 seventy-four heretics from Coventry and Birmingham
were tried, and in 1519 seven were burned, but there is little
evidence of Lollardy in the North in the same period. Professor
Dickens, who has searched the diocesan records carefully, has
found only three cases in the large diocese of York, which covered
Yorkshire, Nottinghamshire and parts of Cumberland, West-
morland and Lancashire, for the period 1500 to 1528, though, as
he says, perhaps the low figure is partly due to the absence
of the appropriate diocesan act books. Wales and the South-
West also seem to have been quite free of the heresy.

Freedom to interpret the Scriptures had in the course of time
given rise to many different and sometimes contradictory
doctrines, some of which Wycliffe would have been the first to
repudiate. Some Lollards said that the Jewish sabbath ought
to be observed and that pork should not be eaten, and others
that pork was a suitable meal for a Friday in Lent. Some said
that a child's baptism was invalid if either the priest or one of the
sponsors was in a state of mortal sin, and some that there was no
sacrament except marriage. But in 1499 there was a report of a
new sect of heretics who declared

... baptism unnecessary for the children of Christians, marriage a
superfluous rite and the sacrament of the altar a fiction.

Such was the diversity of opinion among Lollards that their
name came to be loosely applied to anyone seriously critical of
the Church, including people who refused to pay tithes or coveted
Church lands. It would be wrong, however, to regard every

critic of the Church as such. Since man is a thinking animal, in every age there have been critics among the most devout of churchmen. Some of the best Catholics of the immediate pre-Reformation period found fault in the then existing state of affairs.

Humanism

That revival of learning known as the Renaissance had a profound effect on English scholarship. In Italy, the birthplace of the new movement, renaissance studies had an artistic and literary character; in England, where the people were more deeply interested in religion, as in North Europe generally, its character was primarily moral and religious.

Contact had been established between English scholars and Italian students of the classics before the middle of the fifteenth century, and in the fifties, sixties and seventies the New Learning had some effect on teaching in schools like Eton and Winchester, and in such Oxford colleges as New College and Magdalen. The nature of English education slowly began to change. Till now, with schooling controlled by the Church, the curriculum had been directed to ecclesiastical ends. Elementary education in what were known as A.B.C. or song schools consisted of singing, reading and simple instruction in the Faith. In the grammar school, that breeding ground of priests, the main subjects were Latin grammar and composition, which were taught largely through oral instruction and rote learning, for books were costly and scarce, and these methods were continued in the universities, where dialectic also had its place. Now schools began to be founded where the emphasis was on the study of the classical literature of Greece and Rome, and books were written for use in them which could be 'mass-produced' by printing press.

New impetus was given to the renaissance movement in England when scholars such as Grocyn, Lily and Linacre returned home from their travels in Italy around the turn of the century, and the royal court itself became the resort of scholars, while men of the New Learning began to be found places on the episcopal bench. Grocyn and Linacre, who was to deprive the

Church of its control of the education and organization of the medical profession by getting the King to found the Royal College of Physicians, gave public lectures on Greek at Oxford. Another scholar, John Colet, took a new approach to the study of the Scriptures. The traditional method of the medieval scholars, known as schoolmen, had been to isolate each text and treat it literally and allegorically, and extract from it some spiritual meaning or moral precept, but Colet, in his famous lectures on St Paul's Epistles, tried, by reading the Scriptures in the original Greek, to show the true meaning of them in their historical setting. He sought to discover what the letters had meant to St Paul himself and to those who received them. There were many in the universities who opposed the New Learning, suspecting that the approach of men like Colet could only lead to heresy. They felt their fears justified when, partly as a result of their diehard attitude, the contempt of the Humanists (as the men of the New Learning are called) for medieval scholasticism grew, and with it criticism of the Church as it had developed in the age of the schoolmen, a Church very different from that rediscovered in Colet's re-reading of the Scriptures.

The most famous of English humanists was Thomas More. More was amazingly versatile – scholar, lawyer, diplomat, courtier and wit – but it is his attitude to the Church which concerns us here. He wanted to see the worldliness of the Church replaced by spirituality; he wanted Christianity to be applied to every aspect of life, social, economic and political. In his attitude to Catholic doctrine he was orthodox, ready to defend it with his pen or his life, and, though his eyes were ever open to the Church's abuses, he would not condemn them until he had carefully examined the reasons for them. This was not always true of Colet, and was less so of their friend Erasmus.

Colet became Dean of St Paul's, where he refounded the school, which became a centre of classical scholarship. He attracted vast crowds when he preached. In his sermons he attacked church abuses in a manner not heard from the pulpit since the days of the first Lollard preachers. In his Convocation sermon of 1512 he denounced covetousness as a prevailing temptation among churchmen:

O Covetousness; Paul rightly called thee 'the root of all evil'. For from thee comes all this piling up of benefices one on top of the other; from *thee* come the great pensions, assigned out of many benefices resigned, from thee quarrels about tithes, about offerings; about mortuaries, about dilapidation, about ecclesiastical right and title, for which we fight as though for our very lives! ... from *thee* come burdensome visitations of bishops: from *thee* corruptions of law courts, and those daily fresh inventions by which the poor people are harrassed ... that eager desire on the part of ordinaries to enlarge their jurisdiction; from *thee* their foolish and mad contention to get hold of the probate of wills; from thee undue sequestrations of priests: from *thee* that superstitious observance of all those laws which are lucrative, and disregard of those who point to the correction of morals.

His hearers, all of them clerics, disregarded him.

There was plenty worthy of Colet's attack in his own cathedral, which had long been as much a market place as a place of worship. He tried to reform its statutes but met with opposition from the dignitaries, men with many privileges and few duties, who disliked him for his puritanism and his somewhat contemptuous attitude towards them. He regarded the whole chapter as being in need of correction and drew up new statutes without reference to them, and they refused to ratify them.

Poor Colet's appeals so often fell on deaf ears where the clergy were concerned, but he succeeded in increasing the anti-clericalism of his lay hearers. He also had a good deal of influence on Erasmus to whom he taught the historical method of interpreting the Scriptures.

Erasmus was perhaps the greatest scholar of his day, an Augustinian canon who left the cloister and his native Netherlands to travel the length and breadth of Europe in search of kindred spirits. He certainly seems to have found them in England. He once wrote to an English student studying in Italy:

I have not met with so much learning, not hackneyed and trivial, but deep accurate ancient Latin and Greek, that, but for curiosity of seeing it, I do not now so much care for Italy. When I hear my Colet, I seem to be listening to Plato himself. In Grocyn, who does not marvel at such a perfect round of learning? What can be more acute, profound and delicate than the judgement of Linacre? What has nature ever created more gentle, more sweet, more happy than the genius of More? I need not go through the list. It is marvellous how general and abundant is the harvest of ancient learning in this country.

In his writings Erasmus taught that a man could only be saved if he lived a good life, not by observing forms and ceremonies; and he was apt to make fun of the devotions of the people in a cruel fashion. In his travels around England he came across some odd ceremonies. At St Paul's he saw a stag's head brought to the high altar on the point of a spear to the accompaniment of blasts on hunting horns and a frenzied rabble; really, though Erasmus did not know it, a very odd way of paying rent for twenty-two acres of land in Essex. But St Paul's was the home of something even odder, the shrine of St Uncumber, the bearded virgin who rid women of their unwanted husbands if offerings of oats were made to her. Mixed with the Englishman's true devotion was a great deal of superstition, and there were always crafty clerks ready to make money out of the gullible. At Boxley in Kent there was a mechanical image of Christ on the cross which could be made to bow its head, open its mouth and roll its eyes. To the English peasant with his simple faith the movements of the Rood of Grace were miraculous, and Boxley was an important centre of pilgrimage. One of the most frequented was the shrine of Our Lady of Walsingham. There Erasmus saw what was supposed to be the Virgin's milk; and eleven places in England claimed to have her girdle. At Caversham was 'the holy halter' with which Judas hanged himself, and at Hayles a crystal vase supposed to contain the Blood of Christ shed on Calvary. All these received due reverence from the pilgrim, and the custodians profited from his offering. Never was there more devotion to the saints, and where the Pope would not canonize a famous man, the clergy of the shrineless church where he was buried would. The most popular of the uncanonized saints was

> Master John Schorn,
> Gentleman born,
> Who conjured the Devil into a boot.

There was much in the popular religious life of England for Erasmus to poke fun at. In any case he had a sceptical nature. He did not believe that the doctrine of the Trinity could be proved by Holy Scripture, and confessed that he did not understand the doctrine of transubstantiation. But nevertheless he believed in the authority of the Catholic Church and was willing to obey it.

Influenced by his friend Colet, Erasmus gave the world a new edition of the Greek New Testament together with a new Latin translation, a translation which differed in several important respects from the version approved by the Church, the Vulgate of St Jerome. It was the publication of this *Novum Instrumentum*, rather than Colet's lectures, which turned the attention of the scholars and humanists from the classics to the Bible. Erasmus was the most famous of classical scholars, and other classicists wanted to read his Latin and Greek to improve their own. Among his readers on the continent was one Ulrich Zwingli, and among those in England Thomas Cranmer. It is said that it was reading the *Novum Instrumentum* which turned Zwingli into a reformer. Cranmer had given up the Old Learning for the New when Erasmus had arrived in Cambridge in 1511; now in 1516 he abandoned the law and the classics to study theology. He may have been one of a group of young men who began to meet together in Cambridge's White Horse Tavern to read and discuss the New Testament, and who were very eager to read any book which threw new light upon it.

Lutheranism

Martin Luther was an Augustinian friar, and professor at the University of Wittenberg in Saxony, a man obsessed with his own sinfulness and convinced that nothing he could do would gain him God's forgiveness. Hope of salvation came, however, from his reading of the writings of St Paul, where he found the doctrine that man could be saved only by the grace of God, and not by anything he could do himself. The doctrine of Justification by Faith, a faith, given by God to his elect, in the redemption of the world by Christ in his one and final sacrifice on Calvary, was the core of his teaching. It was not a particularly new idea, for it finds a place in the teaching of St Augustine, but it was bound to cause controversy in an age when the Church laid so much emphasis on the formalities of religion, on the daily offering of Christ on the altar in the Sacrifice of the Mass, on the forgiveness of sins through confessing to a priest and receiving his absolution, and on the remission of the punishment incurred by a sinner through prayer to the saints, through making pilgrimages, through buying indulgences.

It was over the matter of indulgences that Luther first clashed with the ecclesiastical hierarchy. Indulgences had originated in the commutation of penances awarded by a priest after confession into fines where it was difficult for the person who had confessed to perform his penance. As time went on, the indulgence ceased to be a mere fine; it came to be regarded as a means to escape the punishment due to a sinner not only on earth, but also in purgatory, the place where those who have died in the grace of God expiate their sins before being admitted to God's presence. It was claimed that in the course of time the good works of the Church and of the saints had created a 'treasury of merits', credit with God which was far more than they themselves needed for their salvation, and that the surplus could be handed on by the Church to lesser men. We have seen how the English bishops permitted people to sell indulgences to raise money for good causes, much as people sell flags today. In 1517, Archbishop Albrecht of Mainz got the Pope's permission to sell them in order to be able to pay back a loan he had raised to cover the expenses involved in becoming archbishop. Half of the proceeds, however, were to go towards the building of St Peter's Basilica at Rome. Albrecht employed an eloquent agent named Tetzel who persuaded the gullible to buy his indulgences both for their own sakes and for those of their dead friends and relations, with such phrases as 'When the penny rattles in the box, the soul leaps out of purgatory'. Luther was critical not only of the way in which the idea of indulgences was being abused by men like Tetzel and those whose agents they were, but also of the idea itself. He declared that it was not good enough to expect forgiveness by an act of penance; what was needed was penitence for sin. And he nailed his famous Ninety-five Theses on the subject to the door of Wittenberg church so that other scholars at the University could debate them.

This was the beginning of a long controversy during the course of which Luther challenged the infallibility of the councils of the Church, and particularly of that which had condemned the fifteenth-century Bohemian reformer, Huss. In doing this he was thought to be sharing Huss's heresy, and he was excommunicated by the Pope. He now began to publish works attacking the Church's authority. In one of them, addressed *To the nobility of the German Nation*, he claimed that the State had authority over the Church. The Pope's authority was rejected. So, too, in the following year, was transubstantiation, for which Luther substituted a belief similar to Wycliffe's called consubstantiation, a belief that in the Holy Sacrament the bread and wine are present with the Body and Blood of Christ but not combined with them or replaced by them. In the tract in which he attacked transubstantiation, *Of the Babylonish Captivity of the Church*, he rejected the sacraments of Confirmation, Penance, Marriage, Ordination and Holy Unction, claiming that only Baptism and Communion had been ordained by Christ. But his greatest work was something constructive rather than destructive, the translation of the Bible into his own tongue.

Luther's cause was adhered to, largely for political reasons, by the princes of North Germany; his attack on the Church was echoed by others with even less orthodox views such as the Anabaptists, who rejected infant baptism, and Zwingli, to whom the Sacrament of the Altar was merely the outward sign of a spiritually received grace; and these views were picked up by anti-clerical English merchants who brought books containing the new ideas home to England, where there were men eager to receive them. None were more eager than the theological students of Cambridge, those young men who had made the White Horse Tavern their meeting place, obscure men for the present but men whose light was one day to shine bright as they led the

Church as its bishops or died for the new beliefs at the stake, men like Thomas Cranmer, Hugh Latimer, Miles Coverdale and Matthew Parker.

The official attitude of the English ecclesiastical authorities towards Lutheranism was one of condemnation. In 1521 there was a great ceremonial burning of Luther's books outside St Paul's Cathedral, with all the bishops present, Wolsey presiding and Fisher of Rochester preaching. And King Henry himself, after reading *Of the Babylonish Captivity*, published a reply to Luther *In Defence of the Seven Sacraments*, a best seller which, even if, as some historians believe, he only pieced together the research of others, earned him what he had long been seeking from the Pope, a title to match Francis of France's *Most Christian King* and Charles of Spain's *Most Catholic King*. He was now the *Defender of the Faith*.

Despite the official condemnation of Luther's works, the young men continued to meet in their 'local', now known to the rest of Cambridge as Little Germany, and discuss them. And similar meetings were held in Oxford, when some Cambridge men moved there to staff Wolsey's new Cardinal College. In 1523, another Cambridge man, William Tyndale, left England for the Continent, never to return. There he is said to have conferred with Luther and been encouraged to translate the Scriptures into English. The first edition of his New Testament was published in 1525. It and succeeding editions were secretly introduced into England by English and Flemish merchants, some of whom may have helped finance Tyndale's venture. Fear of Lollardy had always led the bishops of the Church in England to take a tougher line than some of their continental brethren and oppose the Scriptures in the vernacular; now the hierarchy forbade the use of Tyndale's version on the ground that it was an inaccurate translation, and that its notes taught false doctrine. More wrote against it; Bishop Tunstall preached against it at Paul's Cross; copies of it were burnt by the public hangman, and those found in possession of it fined or imprisoned. But Tyndale's Cambridge friends not only read it, they distributed it, together with the pamphlets which he produced attacking the Church as a mere human insti-

tution and a barrier between man and the truth of God. Much
of his work, including the notes on his New Testament, were
translations of Luther, and he it was who brought to ordinary
Englishmen knowledge of the great doctrine of Justification by
Faith. Among those happiest to receive copies of his works were
the Lollards, many of whose views had so much in common with
his (though the Lutheran theory of Justification or Solifidianism
was not one of them). The 'Christian Brethren', a mysterious
group who financed the selling of Lutheran books, included
Lollards in their number, and there is a record of how in 1528 a
party of country Lollards from Steeple Bumpstead in Essex
visited the Austin Friars in London and bought from one of
Tyndale's companions of Cambridge days, Dr Robert Barnes, a
copy of his New Testament. Others were visited and preached
to by men who had travelled on the Continent and picked up the
new ideas. At this point it becomes difficult to tell whether the
dissenters tried by the church courts were influenced by the old
heresy or a new one but, while many of the London Lollards
joined forces with the Lutherans, Lollardy seems to have continued as an independent entity for at least thirty years more.

It was in 1528 that Tyndale's first major pamphlet, *The
Obedience of the Christian Man* appeared, and in 1530 it was
followed by *The Practice of Prelates*. On 24 May of that year at a
great gathering of the higher clergy and officers of state with the
King presiding, two hundred and fifty-two passages taken from
the writings of Tyndale and others were read and condemned as
corrupt doctrine. Christians were forbidden to possess such
works and their owners were to surrender them for destruction.
The passages read contained a motley assortment of doctrines.
There was the priesthood of all believers, something subscribed
to by the Lollards; there was Luther's Justification by Faith;
there were attacks on war and secular rulers which the Anabaptists would have approved of.

In a sense this scene goes some way towards summing up
the religious situation in England at the time – the mass of the
people, good faithful Catholics, told what to believe and for
the most part believing; nonconformity already existing among

the common people in the shape of Lollardy, and lately joined by
Lutheranism and other ideas from the Continent, contained in
books which appeal to the growing literate section of the population and particularly the university theologians, feeding upon
and feeding the native anti-clericalism; the hierarchy of prelates
ranking with and sharing the duties of the great officers of state,
and trying to stamp out the growing heresy; and, presiding over
all, the Defender of the Faith, who has already dismissed the
figure so obviously absent from the scene, Thomas Wolsey, and
begun his own subtle attack on the man the Cardinal would have
represented there, the Pope.

Further Reading

For the careers of the various Popes see the appropriate articles in
Encyclopaedia Britannica, and for the Pope's rights in England see
W. E. Lunt, *Financial Relations of the Papacy with England, 1327–
1534* (Harvard University Press, 1962). Information on the bishops
and diocesan administration will be found in Margaret Bowker, *The
Secular Clergy in the Diocese of Lincoln 1495–1520* (Cambridge
University Press, 1968). The lesser clergy are dealt with in that
admirable book by Peter Heath, *The English Parish Clergy on the Eve
of the Reformation* (Routledge and Kegan Paul, 1968), and you will
find information on their education in Joan Simon, *Education and
Society in Tudor England* (Cambridge University Press, 1966). For
Wales see Glanmor Williams, *The Welsh Church from Conquest to
Reformation* (University of Wales Press, 1962). For an Anglican
clergyman's view of the Church on the eve of the Reformation see
H. Maynard Smith, *Pre-Reformation England* (Macmillan, 1965), and
for a Roman Catholic one, volume 1 of Philip Hughes, *The Reformation in England* (Hollis and Carter, 1950). The Humanists are dealt
with in J. K. McConica, *English Humanists and Reformation Politics
under Henry VIII and Edward VI* (The Clarendon Press, 1965), and
the origins of Lollardy in Peter Heidtmann, 'Wycliffe and the Lollards'
in *History Today*, Vol. XX, No. 10 (October 1970). An interesting
collection of Luther's writings, including the 95 Theses, is contained
in E. G. Rupp and Benjamin Drewery, *Martin Luther* (Edward
Arnold, 1970), while the doctrines of Lollardy, Lutheranism and other
Protestant movements are examined in that most readable but not

always accurate little book by Henry Brinton, *The Context of the Reformation* (Hutchinson Educational, 1968). For a scholarly examination of the movements in a particular area see A. G. Dickens, *Lollards and Protestants in the Diocese of York* (Oxford University Press, 1959), and for another scholarly but more general account, William A. Clebsch, *England's Earliest Protestants 1520–35* (Yale University Press, 1964).

PART II
The Break with Rome

[3] THE KING'S GREAT MATTER

The King

He . . . is very religious, hears three masses daily when he hunts, and sometimes five on other days. He hears the office every day in the Queen's chamber, that is to say, vesper and compline.

So wrote Giustiniani, the Venetian ambassador, of the young Henry VIII. Hunting was not Henry's only hobby. Indeed he had so many interests and accomplishments that one wonders how he found the time to enjoy any of them properly. He was a linguist, an able student of mathematics, a composer of some merit; he danced, wrestled, jousted and played tennis, and was a skilful archer as well as a first class horseman. These interests left him little opportunity or inclination for the actual business of governing. He left that to his trusted servant Wolsey, though he would occasionally interfere in matters in which he was particularly interested, and his was the ultimate authority in the realm, his the power to make or break the servants he chose so wisely and discarded so carelessly.

If he did not often find time to attend to affairs of state, he certainly did not neglect his religious duties. But not only did he hear Mass with superstitious regularity, he took a very real interest in the theological disputes of his day. The interest is not surprising even if one does not accept the dubious tradition that if his brother Arthur had not died Henry would not have been King but Archbishop of Canterbury, and that he had been trained for that position. Henry had been brought up in a pious household and he liked to be considered a Humanist; the princes of the Church were his agents and its members his subjects. We have already noted his book against Luther, in which he expressed unshakeable loyalty to the Pope. Some years before, in the aftermath of the notorious Hunne affair, he had taken a rather different line, a line which he was again to follow when the vow of loyalty had been conveniently forgotten.

While attempts were being made to bring Horsey, the Bishop of London's chancellor, to trial for Hunne's murder, the Bishop appointed the Abbot of Winchcombe to preach at St Paul's Cross. The theme of the sermon was the immunity of clergy from lay courts, for the Abbot had recently returned from Rome with a bull which declared that by both human and divine law laymen had no power over clerks. At a time when London was over-whelmingly sympathetic towards Hunne, the sermon was most inappropriate and it was severely censured by the House of Commons. Representations were made to the King who agreed to a debate on the matters it dealt with, in his presence at the Dominican house in Blackfriars. The chief speakers were the Abbot himself and Henry Standish, a noted preacher and Guardian of the Franciscan friary in Newgate Street. Standish opposed Winchcombe with the argument that for three hundred years clerics had been tried in the King's courts; to which the Abbot replied that there was a decree of the Church to the contrary, which all ought to obey under pain of mortal sin. Standish then produced historical evidence to show that no commandment was absolute, some papal decrees having been disregarded even by the bishops. He claimed that no decree of the Church could have any force in England until it had been officially received here. His views brought him a summons to appear before Convocation to answer questions relating to the relative powers of Pope and King in England, and, expecting a charge of heresy, he sought the King's protection. There was a further debate to which bishops, judges and scholars were invited, and in which Standish was supported by the Dean of Exeter, Dr Veysey. The judges then declared that in their opinion Convocation, in citing

Standish, were guilty of *praemunire*, for they had appealed to a foreign jurisdiction in denial of the King's. Shortly afterwards, at Baynard's Castle, Wolsey knelt before the King in the presence of a large company and disclaimed for the clergy any attempt to detract from the royal prerogative. At the same time he begged His Majesty to remember his coronation oath and defend the rights of the Church. It was suggested that the matter in dispute should be referred to the Pope, but the King would not hear of it. He himself gave judgment, and these are the words attributed to him:

By the permission and ordinance of God we are King of England, and the Kings of England in times past had never any superior but God only. Therefore know you that we will maintain the rights of our crown, and of our temporal jurisdiction as well in this as in all other points, in as ample a manner as any of our progenitors have done before our time . . .

Horsey was sent for trial, Standish and Veysey were rewarded with bishoprics and, whether Henry actually uttered those memorable words or not, he had firmly demonstrated his intention to be master in his own house in ecclesiastical matters as well as secular.

The reason for the 'divorce'

The next such demonstration was that which everyone remembers Henry for, the break with Rome. It stemmed out of the King's matrimonial problems, but that it happened when it did was perhaps as much a consequence of the religious climate of the day, of anti-clericalism in England and Protestant schism abroad.

It is not unlikely that the eighteen-year-old Henry married his brother Arthur's widow Catherine of Aragon, an attractive girl six years his senior, for love. It has been asserted that in marrying her he was merely fulfilling his dying father's wish; but the marriage took place in something of a hurry and it involved the abandonment of the old King's diplomatic policy. Henry had in fact been betrothed to Catherine six years before, but her father's failure to send the promised dowry, together

with other political considerations, had enabled other royal
ladies to enter the lists for the prince's hand.

In the happy early days of marriage, Henry showed Catherine
obvious affection, and for most of their time together he treated
her with courtesy and respect. Their happiness was marred,
however, by the fact that Catherine seemed unable to give the
King a son who would succeed him. One boy had been born in
January 1511 but had died within two months, and another,
born in December 1513, died within a few hours of birth. The
only one of their children who survived infancy was their daughter Mary. The future peace of England seemed to Henry to
depend on the succession of a universally acknowledged son and
heir. The days of Lancastrian–Yorkist strife were not so far
behind as to be forgotten; the House of York had its survivors
and its supporters. And nothing seemed as likely to lead to a
renewal of civil war as the accession of a female sovereign.
Queens regnant were unheard of in England. The last attempt
of a woman to succeed to the throne had been made by Henry
I's daughter Matilda back in the twelfth century and had resulted
in years of bloody strife and ultimate failure.

Henry somehow got the idea that the reason for his bad luck
was that God was angry with him for having married his brother's
widow, and it is probable that he had already decided to seek an
annulment of his marriage to Catherine, who had lost her looks
and her strength through frequent, unrewarding pregnancies,
before he met the young girl with the captivating dark eyes,
Anne Boleyn, sometime in 1526. Anne's refusal to grant the
favours he requested outside the marriage bed probably pre-
cipitated the action he took in 1527, but there is little doubt
that the thought was already there. In the book of *Leviticus* was
the commandment 'Thou shalt not uncover the nakedness of
thy brother's wife' and a threat of childlessness for those who
broke it. Henry decided that in view of this the Pope had had
no right to grant the dispensation for his betrothal to Catherine,
that he was not legally married, and that Wolsey and Warham
should try him for incest. His hope was for a verdict of guilty
which would be upheld in Rome. There seemed no reason why

it should not be; doubts had already been cast by theologians on the validity of Julius II's dispensation, and others, including Henry's sister, Margaret of Scotland, had been given decrees of nullity on far less plausible grounds.

The negotiations

Unfortunately for Henry, things did not work out as he had intended. The two prelates delayed giving their verdict on his case in order to seek other opinions, and some of those consulted, among them Bishop Fisher of Rochester, declared that since the Pope had granted a dispensation there was no doubt that the King and Queen were married. Then news arrived that England's enemy the Emperor Charles V had sacked Rome and imprisoned the Pope. Charles was Catherine's nephew, and much as Clement might have wanted to help Henry, who had lately become a fellow member of the anti-Imperial League of Cognac, he was most unlikely to risk the Emperor's wrath by depriving his aunt of her crown.

Convinced of the justice of his case, the King decided to send an agent to Rome to ask the Pope to allow him to marry for a second time without waiting for a legal decision on the validity of his marriage to Catherine. There was a faint chance that Clement would regard bigamy as a lesser evil than 'divorce', but Wolsey thought Henry's move unwise. There was much sympathy for the Queen in England and he felt that marriage to Anne without an annulment was bound to meet with a poor reception from the King's subjects, who would probably be unwilling to recognize the children of the match as legitimate. The Cardinal convinced Henry of the folly of his plan and the agent was therefore told to ask the Pope for permission to submit the case to a legatine court sitting in London. In December 1527, Clement, who had by then 'escaped' from his prison of St Angelo to Orvieto, sixty miles away, agreed that Wolsey and Campeggio, the non-resident Bishop of Salisbury and Protector of England in the papal curia, should preside over the court the King wanted, but he reserved final judgment for himself.

Campeggio, who had probably been instructed to take his time, did not arrive in London till October 1528. He then set about trying to reconcile Henry and Catherine, which he considered to be his first duty. Henry refused to listen, saying that he had been betrothed at twelve to a bride-to-be he had not asked for, and that two years later he had publicly objected to the marriage, as indeed he had, to suit his father's tortuous diplomacy. Campeggio then tried to persuade Catherine to set Henry free by entering a nunnery. This plea, too, fell on deaf ears, the Queen claiming that she had never been anyone's wife but Henry's, for, as the King well knew, her marriage to Arthur had not been consummated. At this the Legate felt inclined to close the case, but Wolsey persuaded him not to. There were further delays owing to the production by Catherine's Spanish friends of a brief Pope Julius had issued with the original dispensation for marriage which answered all Henry's objections to it, and to an attempt to get Clement to declare the document a forgery, which he refused to do without first seeing it.

It was June 1529 before the legatine court met, and soon afterwards the Pope made peace with Charles in the Treaty of Barcelona, one clause of which stated that the court should be dissolved. Wolsey somehow heard of what had happened and tried to hurry things along. But on 23 July, when Henry and his courtiers assembled to hear the judges' verdict, Campeggio, who also seems to have been aware of what was going on in Italy, announced that since his court was part of the Roman Consistory he was bound to observe Roman rules and declare an adjournment for the vacation. A few days later the King was officially informed that Clement had called the case to Rome. He heard too that his ally the King of France, who might have helped his cause, had made peace with the Emperor.

The failure to get an annulment and King Francis's desertion were blamed on Wolsey, the architect of the French alliance, and a man whom Anne Boleyn intensely disliked. On 9 October, the Attorney-General indicted him of *Praemunire* for misusing his legatine authority by, of all things, holding a papal court in England, and two days later he was required to resign the

Chancellor's Great Seal. In the twinkling of an eye the proud prelate ceased to rule England and its Church. Some indication of the way things were going could be seen in Henry's choice of a layman to take over the chancellorship, an office previously held by high ecclesiastics. But what was perhaps even stranger was that Thomas More was not only a layman but a firm opponent of the King's marital plans.

Meanwhile two other of Henry's servants, Stephen Gardiner and Edward Foxe, had told the King of the idea of an acquaintance of theirs, a Cambridge scholar, that he should ask the European universities for their opinion on the legality of his marriage. This appealed to Henry, who thought that support from the universities would give him a lever against the Pope, and he was delighted when his agents, among them his kinsman Reginald Pole, got favourable verdicts from such notable seats of learning as Oxford, Cambridge, Paris, Bourges, Bologna and Padua. However, the reaction of Catherine's Spain was different, as indeed was that of Lutheran Germany. Luther argued that the ban in *Leviticus* on sexual relations with a brother's wife only concerned cases where the brother was still alive, and that Henry had been correct in following an injunction in *Deuteronomy* which bade a man marry his brother's childless widow. Despite these rebuffs Henry was grateful to the Cambridge scholar for his idea, and appreciation of his concern for the royal cause was to put him in the forefront of England's ecclesiastical affairs for the next quarter of a century. His name was Thomas Cranmer.

[4] THE REFORMATION PARLIAMENT

The King and reform

When Campeggio left England in October 1529 his baggage was searched, for there were rumours that he carried with him treasure which Wolsey had given him to put into safekeeping on the Continent, and a papal decree by which Wolsey could legally annul the royal marriage. All that the customs officers found was old clothes and dirty linen. The Cardinal complained of the search as an insult to his position as legate and in reply received a letter in which Henry told him that he had ceased to be legate when the case had been called to Rome. Furthermore His Majesty was astounded

that you are so ignorant of the laws of this realm as to dare to make use of the title of Legate, to which you have no longer any right, for you are a bishop of this realm and you are bound by the most solemn obligation to pay due regard and respect to my royal dignity, my jurisdiction and my prerogative.

The tone was ominous; the royal authority over English ecclesiastics was once more being affirmed. Had Henry already made up his mind to repudiate the papal supremacy should he not get his way over the 'divorce'? It is known that despite official condemnation Lutheran books were circulating at court; Campeggio had himself complained to the King about one which suggested that he and the King of France should 'reduce the ecclesiastical state to the condition of the primitive Church, taking from it all its temporalities'. Then there is some evidence that Anne Boleyn and her friends, though not themselves Lutherans, were trying to influence the King towards Lutheranism and to persuade him to break with the Holy See. Indeed Henry went so far as to defend Luther in a conversation with Chapuys, the Imperial ambassador. He said that although Luther was a heretic he was right to attack the vices and corruption of the Church; the Emperor ought to promote reform as he intended to do himself. He finished by saying that the only power clergy had over laymen was absolution from sin and that even the papal power was severely restricted.

However, there is little clear-cut evidence that in 1529 Henry saw any way out of his marriage to Catherine save through an annulment from Rome. But he had found a new way to put pressure on the Pope. On 3 November a new Parliament met, a Parliament sympathetic to the Queen but with a strong anti-clerical element. They were eager to curtail the exactions and privileges of the clergy, and angry that the Pope's legates had dared to sit in judgment on their King and that the Pope himself had had the effrontery to call his case to Rome. Henry, seemingly carrying out the intention he had intimated to Chapuys, gave Parliament complete freedom to discuss matters of religion. However, he had the power to stop the debate should the Pope see fit to do what he wanted him to.

The Acts of 1529

In the Parliament's first session the Commons introduced legis-lation to deal with a number of clerical abuses and to reduce the fees the clergy received. One of the new Acts reduced probate fees to fixed and moderate proportions. Another fixed the mor-tuary fees on a graduated scale from 17p up to 50p, according to the value of the deceased person's property. When the goods of the deceased were worth less than ten marks and in the case of married women, children, persons who were not householders, and wayfarers, no mortuary was to be taken.

Pluralism and non-residence were attacked in a bill which forbade clergy to take to farm land beyond what was necessary for the support of their household, to keep a brewery or a tannery, or otherwise directly or indirectly trade for gain. Pluralities were forbidden with respect to benefices above an annual value of £8. On the face of it this move to keep the clergy at their pastoral work in the parishes was a worthy one. However, the rich plural-ist was to be a feature of the ecclesiastical scene for many years to come; for, although clerics were forbidden to accept papal licences for pluralities, members of the King's Council were to be allowed to hold three benefices with cure of souls, and chaplains of the King or nobility two. And, although residence was made obligatory, dispensations could be obtained from the King by his and the nobles' chaplains, clerics of noble origin, and doctors and bachelors in divinity or law. Since a large number of existing pluralists fell into these categories, the situation was but little improved; only the poor priest who wished to augment his income by part-time work suffered.

Nor did these Acts have a mollifying effect on the Pope. If they had any effect at all it was the reverse. Clement summoned Henry to appear before the *Rota*, the supreme court in Rome. And then, as if to scotch rumours that he was privately expressing a wish that the King would marry Anne and settle the matter once and for all without involving the Holy See, he issued a series of bulls threatening excommunication if he should do any such thing. He also prohibited anyone from speaking or writing against the validity of Catherine's marriage, and any court or other body from attempting to pass judgment on it.

The pardoning of the clergy

Henry's reaction was to inform the papal nuncio of the existence of the law of *Praemunire*, which declared that those who brought or received papal bulls into England which touched 'our Lord the King, against him, his crown, and royalty or his realm' should be 'put out of the King's protection, and their lands, tenements, goods and chattels forfeited to our Lord the King, and that they be attached by their bodies . . . and brought before the King and his Council'.

In the summer of 1530 he decided to show the world that these were not empty words. Writs of *Praemunire facias* were issued against eight bishops and seven other leading clergy. The charge was that they had aided Wolsey in his offences by handing over part of their income to him. This had indeed happened, but the reason had not been to help Wolsey exercise his papal powers but rather to restrict them. The bishops had bribed him in order to prevent him from overriding their episcopal authority.

Before a decision had been reached in this case, the whole clerical estate were accused of *praemunire*. Although from the existing evidence the charge is not clear, it was probably either one of accepting Wolsey's legatine authority or of exercising their jurisdiction in the Church courts. When Convocation met in January 1531, those who had bribed Wolsey bought off the wrath of the Crown. In return for a pardon, the Convocation of Canterbury agreed to pay £100,000 and that of the much poorer province of York, £18,840. His Majesty's allies, the laity, on the other hand were freely forgiven their *praemunire*. In addition to paying him money, the clergy agreed to acknowledge Henry as their 'singular protector, only and supreme lord ... even Supreme Head', but with the important proviso 'so far as the law of Christ allows'. If this submission was a result of a deliberate campaign to deprive the Pope of all his rights over the English Church (and some would deny that it was) then victory was not yet complete. However, the man who was to be credited with its completion was already on the scene.

Thomas Cromwell

The details of the early career of Thomas Cromwell, the Putney blacksmith's son who was destined to be the much needed replacement for Wolsey at the King's right hand, are somewhat obscure. He had some legal training and worked as a banker in Italy and as a business consultant to English merchants in the Netherlands. He also sat in the Commons of 1523, and must at about that time have entered Wolsey's household. There he was able to rehearse for his star role of the future, involved as he was in the suppression of twenty-nine religious houses to provide for the foundation of the Cardinal's colleges for the clergy at Ipswich and Oxford. On Wolsey's fall he was lucky enough to be elected to the new Parliament as member for Taunton.

It is not known for sure when Henry first became aware of Cromwell's talents. Some believe that it was the part he played in Parliament's anti-clerical debates in 1529 which brought him to the King's notice. Others say that he first attracted the royal attention when he persuaded the Commons to reject the Lords' bill of attainder against his old master, the Cardinal, and gained him a formal pardon under the Great Seal. That was in February 1530; King and future minister were certainly acquainted by the autumn of that year when Cromwell helped Henry replenish the treasury with the revenues of Wolsey's forfeited see of

Winchester, his abbacy of St Albans, and his educational foundation at Ipswich. Before the year was out he was a member of the
royal Council.

Endowed with great energy and vision and a determination to
pursue all he attempted to the bitter end (a quality Wolsey
lacked), this administrative genius quickly showed the King his
worth. After holding a number of lesser offices in the royal
household, he became, in 1533, Chancellor of the Exchequer, and
then in 1534, Principal Secretary. It is probable, however, that
he had been the King's chief minister for some time before getting
either post. Some would credit him with the formulation of
government policy in regard to Rome as early as 1532.

How far that policy was his, however, is a matter of debate.
Professor Scarisbrick feels that the King, who had been so evi-
dently involved in the conduct of affairs between Wolsey's fall
and Cromwell's final ascent, did not allow the latter the freedom
the Cardinal had enjoyed, and that in establishing the royal
supremacy over the Church Cromwell was merely the executant
of Henry's designs. Professor Elton, on the other hand, draws a
clear distinction between the government's tactics of 1529–31,
which he describes as 'unimaginative, bombastic, sterile', and
those of 1532–4, 'direct, simple, successful'. He also says that
Henry was probably kept better informed of what was going on
by Cromwell, but that he exercised a more evident initiative
in government during Wolsey's ministry. This view is supported
by Professor Dickens who feels that it cannot be reasonably
questioned that Cromwell was the guiding force behind the
State–Church revolution of the 1530s. In his opinion, outside
the years 1532 to 1540, when Cromwell was at the helm, the
reign of Henry VIII has scarcely a single creative or revolutionary achievement to its credit.

Certainly it is possible to see Cromwell's mind behind the
events of those years if one wants to. He was no mean scholar;
and his interest in the thought of the day did not exclude Lutheranism. In fact he leaned more in that direction than his King did.
What is more, he was familiar with the work of the Italian
political theorists; perhaps with Machiavelli's *Prince*, certainly

with Marsiglio's *Defensor Pacis*. The *Defensor Pacis* had been published two centuries before, but was a work much in advance of its time. In it, temporal rulers were invested with the sacred task of reforming the Church. That body, according to Marsiglio, was clearly commanded to centre its thoughts and action on the next world; on earth it could claim no rights, property or jurisdiction. He denied that the Pope could claim pre-eminence among the bishops as the successor of St Peter, for Peter enjoyed no such pre-eminence over the other Apostles. And there was no historical proof that Peter went to Rome; the primacy of Rome arose because it was the Empire's capital. Papal decretals and canon law in general had no binding force except with the approval of the State. These theories, first published in England at Cromwell's expense, seemed to be echoed in the legislation of his day; the words of the *Defensor* supported the Reformation Parliament's action.

The Supplication against the Ordinaries

In 1532 the legislative independence of the English Church was destroyed. Ironically, it happened at a time when Convocation was embarking on an impressive programme of reform, issuing canons which put a tighter control on the qualifications of ordinands, attempted to compel clergy to reside, increased the penalties for fornication and imposed a weekly minimum of six hours' scriptural study on incumbents. Such measures, of course, did not please those who wished to see the Church discredited.

The destructive process began with the presentation to Henry by the Commons of their Supplication against the Ordinaries, a document which some scholars believe Cromwell first drafted as an ordinary member of the House in 1529. Its demands for a single sovereignty and undivided allegiance in the realm certainly savour of what are known to have been his views. The draft of 1532 linked together the power of the Church courts, which the Commons disliked, and the legislative power of Convocation, which the Crown wished to control. To some this suggests that the presentation of the document was government inspired. It attacked the power of Convocation to make laws without the consent of the laity. It protested against prosecution over trivial matters in the Church courts, and against high legal fees. It also contained a number of accusations against the Church not connected with the ecclesiastical jurisdiction, including the sale of sacraments and the presentation of minors to benefices, and it criticized the neglect of work through an excessive number of holy days. The clergy made an appeal for the King's protection but Henry's response was to encourage the Commons to continue their attack, and to demand that Convocation should pass no new legislation unless he licensed them to do so. He also insisted that existing canons should be referred for approval or disapproval to a royal commission of thirty-two members, half of them laymen. The following day, he explained to the Speaker and a delegation from the Commons what he had done. He informed them that he had discovered that 'all the prelates at their consecration make an oath to the Pope clean contrary to the oath they make to us, so that they seem his subjects not ours'. Both King and Commons had long been aware of this, but the latter were dutifully horror-stricken, and Henry asked them to consider what might be done. Perhaps fearing the Commons might decide that appropriate action would be the complete destruction of their courts and law-making powers by Act of Parliament, Convocation submitted to the King's demands, and the next day the perceptive Sir Thomas More resigned the chancellorship. Having used the Commons to persuade Convocation to surrender its legislative powers, Henry ignored their other demands.

The Conditional Restraint of Annates

While the Supplication was still being debated by Commons and Convocation, Henry was encouraging the Lords to legislate against annates. The preamble to their bill described them as 'great and inestimable sums of money' which were 'daily conveyed out of this realm to the impoverishment of the same', something we know to have been an exaggeration. It was stated that payments were to cease but that the bill was not to become law until confirmed by letters patent from the King. Henry was trying to bully the Pope into doing what he wished by applying economic blackmail. He had some difficulty in getting both Houses to agree to it. Even the people who had suffered directly from annates, the bishops and abbots, voted against it. Perhaps they still felt some loyalty to Rome; the Commons may have feared reprisals, such as the stopping of the valuable wool trade with Charles V's Flanders. At any rate Henry felt it necessary to be present in the House at the time of the division on the bill. Yet he tried to win the Pope's favour by pretending that he was standing in the way of an all but overwhelming demand by Parliament for the abolition of the payments to the Holy See. He instructed his agents in Rome to 'instil into their ears how incessant have been our efforts to resist importunity of our people from passing the statute'. The Act anticipated retaliation from Rome by declaring that should the Pope delay or deny bulls of consecration, bishops might be consecrated by English authority alone. Should he decide on excommunication or interdict (banning the English people from all ecclesiastical rites), the King and his lay subjects might 'without any scruple of conscience' continue to receive the sacraments and attend the services of the Church.

The Act in Restraint of Appeals

On 23 August 1532 Archbishop Warham died. He had opposed Henry on the 'divorce' question and had made a formal protest against all the Acts of Parliament 'derogatory' to the Pope, to ecclesiastical power and to the privileges of the See of Canterbury'. Now that he was gone Henry had the opportunity to replace him with a man sympathetic to his policy. The man he chose was Thomas Cranmer, by now Archdeacon of Taunton, ambassador to the Imperial Court – and married!

Henry had plans for his protégé. By January 1533 Anne had agreed to share the King's bed and had become pregnant. On or about the 25th of that month they were secretly married so that the expected son and heir would be free from all suggestion of illegitimacy. With an archbishop properly consecrated and granted the authority of *legatus natus*, Henry would be in a position to have his previous marriage annulled in a way which satisfied his desire to abide by 'legality'. And, even if the threats contained in the Act of Annates did not get Henry his 'divorce', they did get from the Pope the necessary bulls for Cranmer's consecration.

A bill was introduced into Parliament to prevent any attempt by Catherine to appeal against the Archbishop's verdict on her marital status to the Holy See; its phraseology has convinced many that the mind behind it was Cromwell's, not Henry's.

... this realm of England is an empire, and so hath been accepted in the world, governed by one Supreme Head and King ... unto whom a body politic, compact of all sorts and degrees of people, divided in terms, and by names of spirituality and temporality, be bounden and owe to bear, next to God, a natural and humble obedience.

These words and those which followed could indeed be said to echo the words of Marsiglio, but the theory that England was an empire or sovereign state was an old tradition based on the legendary descent of the monarch from Constantine the Great. There was a further appeal to the past in a reference to the laws of previous reigns (Provisors and *Praemunire*) which had been designed to keep England 'free from the annoyance as well of the see of Rome as from the authority of other foreign potentates'. These laws had proved insufficient, for they did not cover 'causes testamentary, *causes of matrimony and divorces*, rights of tithes, oblations [donations for pious uses] and obventions [fees occasionally received]'. The 'part of the body politic, called the spiritualty, now being usually called the English Church' was, however, capable of dealing with such matters itself and would in future do so, thus saving the King and his subjects 'great inquietation, vexation, trouble, costs and charges' and preventing 'great delay and let to the true and speedy determination of the said causes'.

The annulment

The Act having been passed (not without resistance from a Commons still worried about the wool trade), further steps were taken to clear the way for the annulment of the King's first marriage. A depleted Convocation passed resolutions that the Pope had had no right to permit the marriage of Henry and Catherine after the consummation of Catherine's marriage to Arthur, and that consummation had been adequately proved. Then on 23 May 1533, at a special court meeting at Dunstable, Cranmer declared the King's first marriage null and void from the beginning. He followed this up with a decree proclaiming Henry's marriage with Anne valid; and the new Queen was crowned. If Henry thought that the Pope would accept the Archbishop's verdict because, as he had stated when giving it, he was 'Legate of the Apostolic See', he was mistaken. Clement's idea of legality was different from Henry's. In July he declared that Anne was not the King's wife, and Henry was excommunicated. However the sentence was suspended till September to give him time to repent and put away his mistress. In that month his daughter Elizabeth was born. Though she was not the boy he had hoped for, she was duly recognized as his heir.

The Act for the Submission of the Clergy

The Pope's attitude resulted in a spate of legislation which, during the early months of 1534, brought the English Church more and more under the royal thumb. One of the new laws put the clergy's submission following the Commons' Supplication of 1532 into statutory form, and the penalty of fine or imprisonment at the King's pleasure was imposed on all who should act contrary to its provisions. Appeals to Rome, which the Act of the previous year had prohibited only in certain cases, were now, under penalty of *praemunire*, forbidden in any case whatsoever. In lieu of the right thus abolished, it was decreed that appeals from the archbishop's court should be made to commissioners appointed under the Great Seal, that is to the King in Chancery.

The Act in Absolute Restraint of Annates

In the previous July the King had put the provisions of the Act of Annates into operation. Now Parliament confirmed his action by passing a new statute which referred to the failure of the 'Bishop of Rome', as the Pope was now called in English official documents, to make use of the opportunity given to him to redress grievances relating to the payments. Not only did the new Act stop the Pope from receiving them once and for all, it also forbade Englishmen to procure papal bulls for the consecration of bishops and abbots. And it confirmed the existing practice whereby the King chose his own bishops, making statutory the attendant formalities. Chapter was obliged to elect the person named in letters missive sent with the *congé d'élire*. Failure to do so within twelve days would cause the chapter to lay themselves open to a charge of *Praemunire*, and the King would then appoint by letter patent.

The Act forbidding Papal Dispensations and payment of Peter's Pence

Another Act, usually called the Dispensations Act, stopped *all* payments to Rome, including Peter's Pence, and said that dispensations allowing departures from canon law should in future be issued by the Archbishop of Canterbury. *Praemunire* featured here too, for its penalties were to be incurred by anyone suing to Rome for any bulls, licences or instruments forbidden by the Act. Strange as it may seem, however, it is possible that even at this late stage Henry was hoping to make his peace with Rome, for the Act was not to take effect until the feast of St John the Baptist, three months later, unless the King should decide to the contrary. In addition the King was empowered to annul the whole or any part of the Act at any time before the feast day. However, that he did not do, for on 23 March 1534 Clement closed the royal case, which had all this time been 'under consideration' in Rome, by solemnly pronouncing Henry's first marriage valid. The immediate answer was a proclamation ordering the Pope's name to be struck out of all prayer books, that it be 'never more (except in contumely and reproach) remembered, but perpetually suppressed and obscured'.

The Act of Supremacy

By the time the first parliamentary session of 1534 ended in that same month of March, the King had an annulment which he found satisfactory, a new wife and a new heir; the Pope had lost all his rights in England except those which he shared with all other bishops, namely his sacramental ones; and the English Church had more than ever been subjected to the royal will. The King's claim to appoint bishops had statutory power behind it; the legislation of the Church was subject to lay approval; its judicial powers were limited by appeal to Chancery. When Parliament met for a second session in November, what this state of affairs really amounted to was recognized in a statute which declared:

Albeit the King's Majesty justly and rightfully is and oweth to be Supreme Head of the Church of England, and so is recognized by the clergy of this realm in their Convocations, yet nevertheless for corroboration and confirmation thereof, and for the increase of virtue in Christ's religion within this realm of England, and to repress and extirp all errors, heresies and other enormities and abuses heretofore used in the same; be it enacted by the authority of this present Parliament, that the King our Sovereign Lord, his heirs and successors, kings of this realm, shall be taken, accepted, and reputed the only Supreme Head in earth of the Church of England.

The first great act of nationalization was over. The King's new title was clearly stated; no allowance was made for convenient consciences with the words 'so far as the law of Christ allows'. However, the Pope had claimed to exercise two kinds of power, entitled *potestas jurisdictionis* and *potestas ordinis*. In this statute the monarch was given *potestas jurisdictionis*, the power to subject the clergy to all the laws of the realm, to define doctrine and ensure the teaching of the same, to hold visitations and reform abuses; he did not have *potestas ordinis*, the right to administer the sacraments, to excommunicate or to preach, for he was not a priest, so he had none of the spiritual powers of a Pope, only the administrative ones. The Church in England might have become the Church of England, but in its hierarchy, its sacraments and its doctrine it remained, for the time being at least, Catholic.

The Act annexing First Fruits and Tenths to the Crown

With the Church firmly under its control, the Crown, impoverished by an active but futile foreign policy and extravagance at court, began to tap its wealth. Though the Act in Conditional Restraint of Annates had condemned those payments to Rome as an 'intolerable burden', they were now made payable to the Crown by all those entering any new living or church office, secular or monastic, high or low. Not only that, but all beneficed clergy were to pay a tenth of their net incomes to the King annually. And he was not going to be content with an assessment made in 1292 as the Pope had been. To make sure he got what he was entitled to, Cromwell, now Henry's Vicar-General in ecclesiastical matters, ordered the compilation of the *Valor Ecclesiasticus*, a detailed account of all clerical incomes. A wonder book of information for the historian, it is the Domesday Book of its time. The result of all this labour was the addition of £40,000 a year to the royal income, though as time went on inflation increased the value of livings and the *Valor*'s assessments, though still applied, became as unrealistic as those of the *Taxatio* of 1292.

[5] APPROVAL AND DISAPPROVAL

The clergy accept the Royal Supremacy

All clergy were required to make a declaration that the Bishop of Rome had 'no greater authority given to him by God in this realm of England than any other foreign bishop', and almost without exception they did. The bishops surrendered their papal bulls and were reappointed to their sees by royal letters patent.

Why did the clergy accept this momentous change so easily? Well, perhaps to many of the poorly educated and untrained lesser clergy the Pope was just a name in the missal, while the power of the King seemed very real. They may not even have understood either the Pope's claims or the King's policy. The Archbishop of York, Edward Lee, informed Cromwell that many of his priests were so unlearned that they could not understand, let alone accept the arguments in favour of the Royal Supremacy. It was perhaps natural that they should follow the example of their better educated fathers-in-God, the bishops.

But why did the bishops themselves accept the change? The question is not an easy one to answer. In his *England under the Tudors*, Professor Elton suggests that because they had been 'battered and badgered' by Wolsey 'they were the less willing or able to resist the demands of the King', that since their administration had been 'disorganized and superseded' during Wolsey's ascendancy, 'they could not hope to marshal opposition when attacked by the laity with the Crown's connivance'. To accept this, however, is to ignore the facts revealed by recent research. Diocesan administration was, in several sees at least, far from disorganized; it did not even suffer as a result of the bishops' non-residence. And it was not superseded; Wolsey might have tried to draw business to his legatine court, but he was too busy with matters of state to attend to the affairs of his own dioceses, let alone to those of other sees.

Dr Elton refers also to the attempt in the previous century, of a constitutional movement in the western Church to replace the Pope's rule by conciliar government. This had not been forgotten and, since Henry had suggested that a general council should adjudicate on his 'Great Matter', it gave him a case in the eyes of men who 'were not over-ardent papalists'. There was much anyway, theologically and legally, claims Professor Elton, to be said on the King's side, at least till 1533.

Another reason he gives for the bishops' submission is that they were in the main the King's servants, used to obeying his commands. Professor Dickens also reminds us of this, and of their training as civil lawyers, when he tells us (in *The English Reformation*) that they were familiar with the claims of the sovereign state, of which the Royal Supremacy was but a translation into real terms. 'The claims of Caesar', he says, 'failed to alarm men nourished upon Justinian.'

These arguments suggest that it was second nature to the bishops to follow the King and abandon Rome. But this is not altogether true. Standish of St Asaph who had upheld the King's prerogatives in the debates against Abbot Winchcombe took up Catherine's cause in the proceedings of 1527. And Veysey of Exeter who had supported Standish in 1516 did not sign a petition for the Pope's consent to the annulment which the Government circulated among the clergy in 1530. Archbishop Warham defied Henry from the beginning, denouncing his tactics in the divorce business in a speech in the Lords. The demands the King made after the Supplication against Ordinaries might have been accepted by Convocation, but the researches of Dr Kelly have shown that the leading opponents of the King's policy were not there when the bishops decided to submit, and that those who were were intimidated by the presence of six lay peers. Apparently the submission was not placed before the Lower House of Convocation, where the deans and archdeacons offered a good deal of opposition to government policy, at all. Then, as we have seen, those whom Professor Elton refers to as 'not over-ardent papalists' voted *en bloc* against the abolition of annate payments to Rome. And the Acts of 1533 which repudiated the Pope's right to allow a man to marry his brother's widow and said that Catherine's first marriage had been consummated were passed by a thinly attended Convocation. Even at this late stage Bishop Tunstall of Durham wrote to Henry, urging him to halt the movement away from Rome, and there is evidence that he was deliberately prevented from attending the vital 1534 sessions of the House of Lords because of his attitude. In the end, as we know, Henry won and the bishops accepted his Supremacy. The reason for this would appear to have been two-fold – firstly, as Dr Scarisbrick has pointed out, the convenient deaths of several of their number who were opponents of royal policy, and secondly fear. There were one or two who would willingly have given the expected answer to Bishop Gardiner of Winchester, whom prudence had lately made the most thorough-going Henrician of them all, when he asked, in his book *De Vera Obedientia*. 'Is John the King's subject only as an inhabitant of England, and the same John not the King's subject as a Christian?' There were probably a good few more who would have agreed with Archbishop Warham, who, as he approached the end of his long life, also decided it politic not to oppose the King, declaring '*Ira principis mors est*', 'the wrath of the King is death'.

The Nun of Kent

Only one bishop opposed the Royal Supremacy to such a degree as to suffer martyrdom for his beliefs. That was John Fisher. The train of events which led to his death started back in 1525 when a poor epileptic servant-girl named Elizabeth Barton began to attract attention with her trances and prophecies. In time a Canterbury monk called Bocking, who was a strong opponent of the royal 'divorce', decided to make use of her against Henry. At his prompting, the Holy Maid or Nun of Kent, as she came to be called, declared that the King would not live six months after putting away Catherine. She claimed that angels had shown her the place in hell prepared for him, and she actually went so far as to force her way into the royal presence to tell him so. She did not long survive this folly. In November 1533, she, Bocking and three accomplices were arrested and made to confess their fraud. In the following April they were executed after a special act of attainder.

This business gave Henry the opportunity to attack some more-important opponents of his policy. Many leading figures of the day had visited or entertained the Nun, among them Fisher and his friend Sir Thomas More. They were both included in the bill of attainder, accused of misprision (that is, concealing their knowledge) of her treason. Fisher claimed he had not reported her prophecies because Elizabeth had told them to the King herself; nevertheless he was fined £300. Thomas More, though very much opposed to the royal 'divorce', had, unlike Fisher, always been doubtful of the genuineness of the Nun's gifts and referred to her as 'the wicked woman of Canterbury'. It was most unfair to include him in the bill, and his inclusion met with strong opposition in the Lords. In the end Henry's councillors persuaded him to leave him out.

Succession and Treasons Acts

During the course of the proceedings relating to the attainder More had revealed his concern for the unity of the Church and his opposition to Henrician nationalism. At the same time, though, he had said that he did not think a Pope to be higher than the general council to which Henry had wished to refer his problem, and that he had done his best to see the King's side in the case, even going so far as to refuse to read the arguments against it. Even so he was regarded as dangerous by a King to whom absolute unity in the state was the prerequisite of civil peace, and Henry seized his chance to put him out of the way.

During that first parliamentary session of 1534 which so weakened the papal power in England, an Act was passed which registered the first of the King's marriages as invalid and the second as valid. It also made it high treason 'maliciously' to deny its validity in writing, print, deed or act, and high treason of course meant the death penalty. Denial in words only, something harder to prove, was regarded as misprision of treason and the punishment was imprisonment and loss of property. Mary was declared illegitimate and the Crown vested in the descendants of Henry and Anne. It was proposed to bind the whole nation to the observance of the Act by oath. When the oath was devised it was used to test the people's acceptance of the Royal Supremacy over the Church, and More failed the test. He was willing to accept the change in the succession but could not accept that England, 'being but one poor member in respect of the whole', could make a valid law against the Universal

Church. Fisher refused the oath too, and both were put in the Tower until an Act was passed which made it possible to commit treason verbally, and verbal treason included 'maliciously' attempting to deprive the King, Queen or their heirs of 'their dignity, title and name of their royal estates'. Fisher admitted that he had said that the King could not possibly be the Supreme Head on earth of the Church of England, but claimed he had spoken in confidence and without malice. Malicious or not, he whom Pope Paul III misguidedly made a cardinal in May, was in June beheaded at Tyburn. A fortnight later, on 6 July 1535, More followed him to the block.

Observants, Carthusians and Bridgettines

Though in general the clergy, monastic and secular, agreed to accept the Royal Supremacy without a struggle, there were three groups of them who did not. They were the Carthusians and the Bridgettines of Syon in Middlesex, both of them very strict and zealous orders, and the Observant Friars. Henry attacked the Observants first because, as itinerant preachers, they were in a position to do him the most harm. A number of them were imprisoned, the rest fled the country and their seven houses were appropriated to the Crown. The Carthusian and Bridgettine leaders were then arrested, tried in a secular court and condemned. The priors of the Charterhouses (Carthusian monasteries) at London, Beauvale in Nottinghamshire and Axholme in Lincolnshire, and a priest from Syon were all hanged, drawn and quartered on the same day. Three other leaders of the London Charterhouse were tortured for a fortnight in Marshalsea Gaol before they too were butchered. Other inmates gave in, as did the Bridgettines, and took the oath, while the rest, ten in all, were chained up in Newgate Prison and left to die. Why was there such a difference between the way in which More and Fisher were treated and the fate of those other opponents of the royal will? Why gentle persuasion for the one and fiendish torture for the other, a quick and comparatively painless death for the one and a slow, agonizing one for the other? Perhaps it was

because Sir Thomas and the Bishop were respected public
figures with a personal following, while, as Professor Elton has
said, 'no one had any patience with monks', however devout.

Further Reading

For a thorough and straightforward account of the 'divorce' proceedings see J. J. Bagley, *Henry VIII and his Times* (Batsford, 1962),
and for a scholarly chapter on the intricacies of the canon law concerning the 'divorce', J. J. Scarisbrick, *Henry VIII* (Eyre and
Spottiswoode, 1968). G. R. Elton's *Henry VIII, an essay in revision*
(The Historical Association, 1962) is largely a discussion of how far
the King formulated his own policy and ran his own government, and
how far this was the work of Wolsey and Cromwell. For Cromwell's
career see A. G. Dickens, *Thomas Cromwell and the English Reformation* (English Universities Press, 1959). You will find extracts from
the Acts of the Reformation Parliament in A. G. Dickens and Dorothy
Carr, *The Reformation in England to the Accession of Elizabeth I*
(Edward Arnold, 1967). For matters relating to the membership and
management of that Parliament see another volume in this series,
R. K. Gilkes, *The Tudor Parliament* (University of London Press,
1969), and for a detailed account of its activities, S. E. Lehmberg,
The Reformation Parliament 1529–36 (Cambridge University Press,
1970). You will find relevant articles in the various historical journals,
for example M. Kelly, 'The Submission of the Clergy' in *Transactions
of the Royal Historical Society*, 5th series, XV, 1965. Perhaps the best
book on More, though sympathetic to its subject, is Raymond W.
Chambers, *Thomas More* (Jonathan Cape and Penguin, 1963).

Principal Events

1503. Julius II grants dispensation for Henry and Catherine's betrothal
1509. Henry's accession and marriage
1515. Debate on clergy's immunity from secular courts
1521. Henry's book *In Defence of the Seven Sacraments*
1527. Henry starts 'divorce' proceedings. Charles V imprisons Pope
1529. 18 June. Legatine court begins to try Henry's case
23 July. Court adjourns. Case recalled to Rome
11 October. Wolsey dismissed
3 November. Reformation Parliament meets. Acts reducing probate and mortuary fees and attacking pluralities and non-residence
1531. Submission of the clergy
1532. Convocation makes reforms. Supplication against Ordinaries. Act in Conditional Restraint of Annates
1533. January. Henry and Anne marry
March. Cranmer Archbishop. Act in restraint of Appeals
May. Cranmer annuls Henry's marriage to Catherine
July. Henry excommunicated
September. Elizabeth born
November. Nun of Kent executed
1534. January to March. First parliamentary session. Acts for the Submission of the Clergy, in Absolute Restraint of Annates, forbidding Papal Dispensations and payment of Peter's Pence. Succession Act. Pope closes Henry's case
November. Second parliamentary session. Act of Supremacy. Act annexing First Fruits and Tenths to the Crown. Treasons Act
1535. May. Leading Carthusians executed
June. Fisher executed
July. More executed

PART III
The Henrician Church 1536-47

[6] THE DISSOLUTION OF THE MONASTERIES

Monastic England

In 1530 there were at least 825 religious houses in England and Wales. 502 were houses of monks (usually called monasteries), 136 were nunneries, and 187 were friaries. The monks included Benedictines, Carthusians, Cistercians and Cluniacs, as well as members of more obscure orders such as the Grandimontines and the order of Tiron with one house each in England and Wales. Some religious were called canons and followed the more flexible rule of St Augustine which allowed them to do much good work away from the cloister, particularly in the hospitals. Some canons followed the reformed rule of Premontré, others were Bonhommes, and others members of that exclusively English institution, the double order of St Gilbert of Sempringham with sisters as well as brethren. There were members of both sexes too in Syon Abbey, England's only Bridgettine house. Elsewhere nuns were supposed to follow the rule of St Benedict, St Bernard or St Augustine without the benefit of male company.

The Friars Minor of St Francis (the stricter variety of whom were called Observants) and the Friars Preacher of St Dominic took their faith out into the world, preaching the Gospel. They and their colleagues of the Carmelite and Augustinian orders seldom resided for long in one house. Their friaries were less homes than ports of call. The brethren of St John of Jerusalem followed their vocation in hospitals, where it was for the sick to command and for them to obey.

There were perhaps 7,500 men and 1,800 women altogether who were bound by the three-fold vow of poverty, chastity and obedience, and bound, too, to pray for their founders and bene-factors and to give alms and hospitality to those who needed them. They must have been a most noticeable feature of the English scene when the total population was only 3½ million.

Who were these people who chose the common life? The monks were mainly of peasant stock. Some were sent into religion against their will by ambitious parents who wanted to save them from the ploughman's toil; others took their vows gladly as the entry fee to a life of contented ease away from the troubles and hard-ships of the outside world. The nunneries were often the homes of gentlewomen whose families declined to support them in their spinsterhood. The names of some of the richest families in Devon – Carew, Pollard, Coplestone, Fortescue, Ayshford, Sydenham, Fowell, Pomeroy and Kelly – were borne by inmates of Polsloe and Canonsleigh priories in the 1530s. Those of either sex who sought to lose themselves in spiritual exercise were perhaps comparatively few. Indeed it was very difficult to culti-vate spirituality in a rich community where time had inevitably to be devoted to the administration of the accumulated wealth of centuries, and where the superior was expected to behave more as a feudal magnate than as a father-in-God.

Some of the religious lived in magnificent abbeys, some in priories sometimes even more magnificent, others in small cells with one or two of their fellows. By the sixteenth century, the title of a house did not depend upon size so much as upon the custom of its order. At one time the prior had always been the abbot's deputy as the head of the monastery, but from the foundation of Cluny in the tenth century the heads of daughter houses of that abbey had been termed priors, and their institu-tions priories. Later, canons-regular, Carthusians and Domini-cans all gave the title of prior to the heads of their houses, and the daughter houses of English Benedictine abbeys were called priories. Monastic cathedrals were priories too, for, although the bishop had the right to preside in chapter as the titular abbot, the prior ruled the monks.

Thirty abbots and priors ranked with the bishops as Lords Spiritual and had voting rights in the House of Peers. Like the bishops they served the King as justices of the peace, presiding over courts, surveying roads and bridges, and licensing ale-houses. Then, too, they served on special commissions to deal with particular emergencies in their home territories, where their monasteries were often the principal landlords and employers of labour. Farm labourers, shepherds, gardeners, smiths, huntsmen, barbers, waiters, laundry women and dairy maids all figured on the monastic payrolls. All in all, the servants greatly outnumbered their masters. At the famous Yorkshire abbey of Rievaulx, for example, there were 22 brethren of the Cistercian order and 102 'servants'.

Monastic wealth

Collectively the religious houses were very rich. According to the *Valor Ecclesiasticus*, their total income was over £160,000 a year, perhaps forty times that in the money of our own day, twenty-eight houses each having a gross income of over £1,000. The richest was the Benedictine abbey of royal Westminster with £3,912 a year. At the other end of the scale were those 9 per cent of religious houses with an annual income of less than £20.

Several of the very rich monasteries were important centres of pilgrimage and had a reasonable income from what may be termed the tourist trade. Money came, too, from other 'spiritual' sources, from the tithes of appropriated parishes and from rents paid for glebe. Land was the biggest source of monastic revenue. There has been much debate as to how much land the religious orders really did own. Simon Fish claimed that the *clergy* owned a third of England, and later writers took this figure to apply to monastic lands alone. Recent estimates of monastic property have varied from one-sixth to one-twentieth of the realm.

The monks did not farm or mine much of their land themselves; much of it was let out to rent, as were their manorial cornmills. Very often the demesne land around the monastery was all they retained for their own use. We know, however, that some houses sold the timber from their estates, and others exploited the natural wealth which lay in the rivers flowing through them, building weirs and depriving estuary fishermen of their livelihood.

Being manorial landlords the monks were entitled to receive the usual manorial dues, such as heriots and amercements, and the profits of manor courts. Sometimes they had the right to collect market and fair tolls from the towns on their estates, though their attempts to assert such a right occasionally led to trouble, even violence, from the townspeople.

In view of the wealth of the monasteries, perhaps it is not surprising that an impoverished Crown, having nationalized the Church, should decide to take some of that wealth for itself. After all, the monastic income was more than three times the income from all the royal estates. We need look no further than this for the reason why, in 1536, an Act was pushed through Parliament for the dissolution of the lesser houses. The Government had less than enough to meet the increasing costs of internal administration and of defence against a possible attack from foreign critics of the Church settlement. Whatever money the Sovereign's father had left, if indeed he had left any at all, had been consumed in futile European warfare, and parliamentary grants were too infrequent and too small to be relied upon.

It is still a popular thesis that the monasteries were dissolved because they were hot-beds of Popery, because the monks were, in Professor Elton's words, 'less national than the secular clergy and owed a special duty to Rome'. Now it is true that the English bishops' powers of visitation were limited to houses of Benedictine monks and nuns, Cistercian nuns and Augustinian canons, and that even some of the larger Benedictine houses were subject directly to Rome. In general, however, the houses exempt from episcopal visitation were not in special obedience to the Pope but to continental mother houses which appointed visitors to inspect them, and by the sixteenth century these visitors were as a rule English abbots and priors of the exempt orders. In any case the abbots were, as we have seen, the King's servants, and, moreover, the Crown was the founder or patron of countless abbeys and priories and nominated their superiors. The monasteries of the 1530s were English houses of English monks, who, when their turn came, generally took the Oath of Supremacy without demur. We cannot deny the religious orders their martyrs, but we can point out that those who died did not all die because they rejected the royal supremacy. And then not all the martyrs the monasteries produced died in Henry's reign; some, like the ex-Cistercian John Hooper, died in Mary's reign for professing beliefs neither Henry nor the Pope would have agreed with. Moreover, we have only to see how many of their brethren got rich parishes, deaneries and even bishoprics, not just in the time of 'Catholic' Henry but in the reformed Church of Elizabeth's day, to realize that it was in the monastic cloister that the Crown found some of its staunchest supporters. It is difficult, therefore, to accept Dr Elton's argument that the dissolution took place because the Government 'could not risk a monastic revival in favour of the pope'.

Evidence of laxity

The excuse offered by the Crown for the dissolution was not Popery, but the failure of the professed to perform their religious duties and to live up to Christian ideals. Now since to err is human, it is natural in any human society to find people who do not quite reach the standard expected of them, and inevitably this was so in the monastic cloister. There were those monks and nuns who forgot their vow of poverty and lived the life of country gentlefolk, eschewing the coarse habit of their order for the fashionable dress of the court; there were those for whom chastity had no appeal and who were not without their mistresses and lovers; there were those who were far from obedient to their superior or to the rules of their order. Not all of them said the eight daily offices, and those who did were sometimes slovenly in their approach. We know all this because records survive of regular visitations made to the religious houses by the diocesan bishops, and also of the injunctions left by the bishops ordering the inmates to remedy their faults. In some places they reveal a truly shocking state of affairs; in others (and this perhaps is what really should surprise us, considering the distractions from the spiritual life) discipline was kept and everything was in order.

Some idea of the sort of situation a bishop found in a less than perfect house can be gathered from the injunctions sent to two houses, one of nuns and the other of monks, by their diocesan bishop after a visitation in 1521. Writing to the Prioress of Cornworthy, Devon, in English, 'the rather by you to be understood', the Bishop of Exeter commanded her to see that divine service was said at the appointed time, in the appointed place, and in the appointed manner, by the whole convent (except where the nuns were too old or sick to go to chapel) 'as in other devout places of your religion it is observed and kept'. He ordered the sisters to sleep together in the same room and to eat together. He forbade them to wear 'pompous apparel', inhibited them from receiving guests without his licence, and told them to inform servants surplus to their needs that their services would no longer be required. Then he requested them to keep their three vows. That she might rather give herself 'to the contemplation and religious conversation' he ordered the Prioress to stay in her house and not to deal personally with 'any outward husbandry, wandering in the fields and other prophane places irreligiously out of the priory', but to leave necessary contact with the outside world to 'some discreet, virtuous man'.

Later the Bishop sent a similar set of injunctions to the Prior of Tywardraeth in Cornwall. This time he wrote in Latin. He complained that the divine office was not being said and that silence was not being observed in the cloister. He ordered the brethren to say matins shortly after midnight 'prout in aliis domibus vestre religionis observatur', and that silence be enforced after compline. He had heard that the brethren were coming and going from the monastery without reasonable cause, and therefore forbade them to leave without a licence. The Bishop then turned to the vow of chastity. He ordered all doors, windows and other places 'quibus mulieribus ad eos pateat introitus vel fratribus tuis ad eas exitus' to be blocked up within two months. Next he complained that they had broken their vows of poverty. He requested the Prior to make them give up their private fortunes and to make sure that no monk received more than £5 a year for his victuals and clothing.

Such a situation was by no means new. Episcopal visitation had been resulting in this sort of injunction for centuries, just as it had been resulting in praise for well-ordered houses. However, the Crown made corruption in the cloister its excuse for the dissolution of the smaller places of religion and took pains to produce a singularly black picture of life therein to support its case.

Lay interference in monastic affairs

One of the reasons why the monks were unable to get on with their religious duties in the way they should was the disruption caused by the interference of laymen in their monasteries' lives. Sometimes influential laymen were given the usually nominal position of steward of a monastery's estates and a handsome salary so that their influence would be exercised locally and at court in the house's favour. Cromwell himself held a number of such posts. The stewards profited in more ways than one; they were able to become well acquainted with the monastic estates, and when, after the dissolution, the Crown put them on the market they knew which parts were the most profitable and most worth bidding for. Some of them did do some service for their employers. For instance, the Prioress of Nuneaton had Lord Dorset to protect her against her rebellious tenants. More often, however, the stewards seem to have been more of a nuisance than a help, regarding their office as an excuse to interfere in a house's internal affairs. The same can be said of many of those country gentry who held the position of receiver of rents or auditor of accounts, and of those who bought themselves the right to a pension from a monastery or were given it in return for support. Some of them got clothing and free board and lodging from the houses they served, and it was therefore important to them that they should be well-run and in good financial order. Some went so far as to interfere in elections to get an abbot or prior who would rule in their interests.

The prime interferers in monastic affairs (apart from the Crown) were the founders or patrons, the descendants of those who had originally been responsible for the foundation of the convents, or of those who had bought the title of founder and the rights which went with it. The founder had the first claim to the prayers of his house; he also had the right to free board and lodging there whenever he paid a visit, and the right to be buried in the choir of the brethren's church. He could, and sometimes did, demand a visitation if he was dissatisfied with the way in which his monastery was being run; and the community had to ask his permission to elect a new head. Some patrons even did their best to force a resignation from a superior who proved unsatisfactory.

The Crown was the most powerful of founders. Most of the ancient abbeys had been founded by kings and many others had passed into royal hands through marriage, attainder or confiscation. Mr Baskerville has described the Crown as 'the arch-interferer in the economy of the religious houses'. As it was the founder of so many houses it was inevitable that this should be so. Its agents frequently took the administration of the monasteries out of the hands of the monks in order to protect its financial interests, and the abbots, who, as we have seen, often performed public service for the Crown, were elected on the receipt of a *congé d'élire*. By the 1530s Cromwell was interfering in financial affairs and elections at monasteries other than those in the Crown's patronage. Not only did his nominees wear the abbatial mitre, his clients gained very profitable leases, offices and grants from the religious houses. The religious orders were well under the Crown's thumb before the dissolution begun.

The Royal Commissions

Much of the Crown's intervention in monastic affairs was done by letter, but once the Act of Supremacy had endowed the King with powers of visitation, the monks were subjected to a number of royal commissions. First came that which drew up the *Valor*. Its members were familiar to the religious. They included not only the higher clergy of their diocese, whom they would be used to seeing on visitation, but their own employees, those local gentry who were the stewards, receivers and bailiffs of their estates – a very sensible choice of Crown agents in this case, for they were well able to provide the Government with an account of what it would gain once the monasteries had been shut down.

Dr Woodward believes that it was the receipt of the returns of the *Valor* commissioners which made the Government decide to dissolve all religious houses with an income of less than £200 a year. 'They could see', he says, 'that to adopt this dividing line would provide the crown with a comfortable endowment without antagonizing any of the more powerful religious interests.'

The next royal agents the monasteries had to entertain came on a visitation of the traditional sort – traditional, that is, except for the fact that they were acting on the orders of the King's Vicar-General, the layman Thomas Cromwell. (The Abbots of Stanley and Forde had already been ordered to visit the Cistercian houses, but there is no record of this visitation ever having been carried out.) What the visitors discovered is recorded in letters sent to Cromwell and in the *Compendium Compertorum*, the book of findings produced by the visitors of the northern monasteries, Drs Layton and Legh, and perhaps the original of the 'Black Book' of legend. Using the same sort of questionnaire as the episcopal visitors, but concentrating on offences against the vow of chastity, for they were the most likely to shock, Layton and Legh produced a far more damning picture of life in the religious houses than the bishops ever had. Indeed there are some curious discrepancies between the reports of the royal visitors and the injunctions of their episcopal counterparts issued shortly before. In 1532 Bishop Richard Nix had held a visitation of his diocese of Norwich. It is possible to compare the report of the King's visitors with his findings in eighteen cases. The visitors looked for and found lapses of sexual morality in all but one of the houses, the Bishop at only one. And they found twenty-one offenders in seven houses at which the Bishop had said all was well. Perhaps the lapse of time between the Bishop's visitation and that of the royal agents accounts for this change. But then in some cases there is a remarkable difference between their report and that of the commissioners responsible for the actual dissolution made just a few months later. For example at two places in Leicestershire where the visitors had complained of serious lapses in behaviour, the suppression commissioners found things to their satisfaction.

Much that is critical, indeed damning, has been written about the visitors, and especially about Legh and Layton. They have even been accused of fabricating the monks' crimes in order to provide an excuse for dissolution. Professor Knowles, however, feels that the visitors were not as bad as they have been painted, indeed no worse than any of the other government agents of the time. They could be unscrupulous if it was necessary to be so in order to keep the King's or Cromwell's favour, but were often 'sagacious, moderate and good-natured in their personal dealings when neither career nor cash was at stake'. Professor Dickens does not believe their account of monastic shortcomings to have been deliberately fabricated, but explains that the reason why it was such a black one was that 'by a novel perversion of the traditional [visitation] procedure, evidence was now taken from witnesses outside the cloister, many of whom may have been inspired by personal grudges, by rumours and modish tendencies to anticlericalism'. How Legh and Layton managed to interview all the monks and nuns in a hundred and twenty houses, and outsiders as well, between 22 December 1535, the earliest date at which they could have started their progress through the North, and 28 February 1536, when they claimed to have finished, is hard to imagine.

The fall of the lesser houses

In the Spring of 1536, Parliament passed an Act for the dissolution of all religious houses (except friaries) with a net income of less than £200 a year, the excuse being that the smaller monasteries were places of 'manifest sin, vicious, carnal and abominable living', the evidence probably that collected on the royal visitation. Their inmates were to be transferred, if they so wished, to the greater houses of their orders, where 'religion is right well kept and observed'. Nothing could have been further from the truth if the visitors' reports were to be believed, for they painted a worse picture of the large abbeys than of the smaller places of religion.

The new Act was not entirely without precedent. When Henry V had renewed the Hundred Years' War he had ordered small monasteries in England which were dependent on mother houses in France to sever their links with the Continent or suffer dissolution. Sometimes bishops had dissolved religious houses to provide funds for other purposes. John Fisher, for example, had received papal permission to suppress two nunneries in order to found St John's College at Cambridge. On the Continent, Gustavus Vasa of Sweden and the Lutheran princes of Germany were among those lining their pockets with monastic wealth.

The dissolution was not altogether unexpected. When, years earlier, Bishop Fox of Winchester had been considering attaching his new college of Corpus Christi at Oxford to a monastery, Bishop Oldham of Exeter had tried to dissuade him with the now famous words:

What, my lord, shall we build houses and provide livelihood for a company of bussing monks, whose end and fall we may live to see; no, no, it is more mete a great deal that we should have care to provide for the increase of learning, and for such as who by their learning, shall do good in church and commonwealth.

The general apathy among so many inmates of the monasteries, and growing doubts about what useful purpose they served must have led many to feel that their days were numbered.

Despite its terms, the Act of 1536 did not actually mark the end of all those religious houses with an income of below the stipulated £200 per annum. Ninety-two cells of larger monasteries were regarded as part of their mother houses because they were not separate entities in the administrative sense. The Gilbertine houses, seventeen in number, were also allowed to survive, perhaps because their Master, Robert Holgate, was a friend of Cromwell's. Another sixty-seven convents also gained exemption, in some cases by making a generous gift to the Vicar-General, so only 243 out of a total of 638 houses of monks, canons and nuns were dissolved.

What happened to the monks, canons and nuns? Some of them moved to the larger houses as the Act had intended – 95 per cent in Yorkshire, but as few as 25 per cent in Norfolk. As many as 975 monks and canons asked the suppression commissioners for or were forced to take capacities – dispensations which released them from their vows of poverty and obedience, and enabled them, with a grant of twenty to thirty shillings to tide them over, to take up employment as secular clergymen or to seek a lay occupation. The nuns, whose chance of a livelihood outside the cloister was limited, usually chose to cling to the veil, and thereby created accommodation problems for which exemptions from suppression were the only cure.

Abbots, priors and prioresses were luckier than their humbler brethren and sisters. Unlikely to accept an inferior position in another convent, they were granted pensions roughly proportionate to the incomes of their houses. An effort was also made to ensure that monastic servants and people dependent on the monks for their living did not suffer as a result of the suppression. All future occupants of monastic houses, and people purchasing or renting monastic property from the Crown were required to maintain

an honest continual house and household in the same site or precinct, and to occupy yearly as much of the same demesnes in ploughing and tillage of husbandry, that is to say, as much of the same demesnes which hath been commonly used to be kept in tillage by the governors, abbots, or priors of the same houses . . .

so that hospitality and arable farming did not decay, and there would be as little unemployment as possible.

Not only were the low-born servants protected, but the high-born too. The country gentry had a lot of influence in the House of Commons so they kept their annuities as stewards and pensioners of the monasteries and their leases as occupiers of monastic property. However, all grants of fees, annuities and leases made within a year before the passing of the Act were to be subject to close scrutiny, for rumours of impending dissolution had led to sharp practice. Abbots and priors had begun to provide for their own and their relations' futures by drawing up long-term leases and making grants of church patronage to their friends and kinsfolk. On 25 October 1535, Abbot Tucker of Buckland had leased the rectorial tithes of St Andrew's Church, Buckland to his brother Robert and his nephews William and Hugh for sixty years.

When the monks left, the suppression commissioners usually put a monastery into the hands of a local man who was willing to rent (or *farm*) the property. Moveable goods, such as gold and silver plate, were sent up to London, while household chattels and livestock were put up for sale locally, and usually passed to the farmer. Vestments were sometimes put to new and profane use as bed covers, while bells were turned into cannon, and lead from the roof was melted down and recast into pigs which were sent to the capital or exported to the Netherlands. The overall supervision of monastic property was the task of the Court of Augmentations, set up by Cromwell in April 1536, though in Lancashire it was the concern of the Duchy of Lancaster authorities. It was these bodies which sold or leased that property for the enrichment of the Crown.

Resistance to dissolution

In general the dissolution went smoothly, though there was some resistance from the Augustinians of Hexham in Northumberland and of Norton in Cheshire. At the Benedictine priory in Exeter, which was famous for its charity, it was the local women who caused trouble. They attacked the workmen who were taking down the rood, one of whom broke a rib by jumping from a window to try and escape them.

The Pilgrimage of Grace, so often associated with the dissolution, was not just a pro-monastic rising. The dissolution was simply the last item on a growing list of grievances in a conservative area of the country which resented the increasing interference by the central government in a land of ancient liberties and feudal allegiances. Among the things which troubled the rebels were the collection of a lay subsidy, and a rumour stimulated by this and the Act of Annates that the King intended to confiscate all the gold in the country. Enclosure, too, played its part, and so did the tale that no one would be allowed to eat white bread, pigs or capons without a licence.

The sight of the suppression commissioners turning out monks and carting the treasures of their monasteries off to London led the people to fear that the parish churches which they themselves had enriched with their gifts would be the next to be plundered. To deep-rooted political and economic grievances were added religious ones. The rebels, who rose first in Lincolnshire and whose torch was taken up by the Yorkshiremen, wanted an end to the dissolution and heretical bishops like Cranmer and evil counsellors like Cromwell to be dismissed from their posts. They and not the King were held responsible for all the country's troubles.

It was Robert Aske, the leader of the Yorkshire rebels, who designated the rebellion a pilgrimage and chose the banner of the Five Wounds of Christ as its standard. He not only wanted the monasteries to be restored, but the Pope's authority too, and, dissatisfied with the legislation of the Reformation Parliament, he called for the election of a new one free from royal interference. Not all the rebels agreed with him on the matter of the papal supremacy. He himself said that the main reason why they followed him was because they feared a drain of currency – of which they had but little – to the non-resident southern landlords who might succeed the monks. After some persuasion from their leader, they agreed, however, that the King should not exercise any spiritual powers, even that of visitation, though he might retain the title of 'Head of the Church'.

How dangerous a rebellion was the Pilgrimage of Grace? To Professor Dickens the events of 1536-7 formed the major crisis of the Tudor dynasty. Dr Scarisbrick feels that the rebels were in a position to 'swamp' the King, but that they made the mistake of allowing their leader to dissuade them from marching south and making conquests. To Aske they were pilgrims not rebels; their purpose was to plead with Henry to grant their requests, not to gain them by force. He persuaded them to trust their Sovereign. Henry promised them a northern parliament to deal with their complaints and a free pardon, and they all went home. Since the promises seemed a long time in being fulfilled, there was a further outbreak and the leader now was Sir Francis Bigod, an advanced Protestant, who objected to the Royal Supremacy on different grounds to Aske's. No mortal, he believed, could occupy a position which was rightfully Christ's. The new trouble led to brutal repression by the royal forces and death for Aske and other leaders.

At one point, apparently, the rebels had contemplated seeking the Emperor's aid, and the Holy See itself had been prepared to intervene. Reginald Pole had been made a cardinal and sent to Flanders to call on Henry to repent and submit, and perhaps to raise an army to support the insurgents. But he went too late; by the time he arrived in Flanders the rebellion had been put down. Perhaps it was hoped that his presence just across the Channel would encourage the North to take up arms and the Cross again, and that he would gain the assistance of either Charles V or Francis of France. Such assistance was not forthcoming. Both Francis and Charles hoped for Henry's help in the war between them. Dr Scarisbrick thinks that had things been just a little different Henry's reformation might have been undone and his place taken on the throne by his daughter Mary, possibly as Pole's bride. Dr Parker, however, believes that the northerners were far too loyal to the throne ever to support a foreign invasion, and that the rising was too local, too far from the centre of government, to have much chance of seizing power.

As the urge to rebel had spread throughout the northern counties, dispossessed monks and nuns had been put back into their houses. Perhaps sixteen out of fifty-five convents in the

North had come back to life. In the hour of defeat some of the monks claimed that they had been forced back against their will. This plea did not prevent the Abbot of Sawley from being condemned for treason, but there is no record of his having suffered the death penalty. The Prior of Cartmel avoided the temptation to treason by fleeing to the royal camp.

In Lincolnshire the rebels had looked to the greater abbeys for support. They had had to threaten to burn Kirkstead and Barlings abbeys to the ground before they had got any help from them. Even so, their abbots died as traitors. When the Yorkshire pilgrims had marched through the county's capital they had insisted on the Abbot of St Mary's walking at the head of the procession, carrying his house's processional cross. He had reluctantly agreed but had withdrawn at the earliest opportunity.

The heads of some houses like Byland, Whitby and Bridlington contributed to rebel funds. The Abbot of Kirkstall even attended a rebel meeting in Pontefract. They were men who enjoyed a rich living and would have been reluctant to lose it; papalism should not necessarily be regarded as their motive.

The Prior of Bridlington was eventually executed, though he claimed to have been bullied into giving support, as did his fellow 'martyr', the Abbot of Jervaulx, who had actually given the rebel leaders hospitality in his house and, at their leave-taking, fled to Bolton Castle to avoid getting into their clutches again. A former Abbot of Fountains suffered because he had been staying at Jervaulx when the rebels called. The Abbot of Whalley died for a number of crimes, including giving shelter to one of the monks of his rebellious neighbour at Sawley. Lesser religious from Bardney, Cartmel, Louth Park and Whalley also suffered the supreme penalty.

The reinhabited priories were re-emptied. The greater houses whose heads had been found guilty of treason were treated as though they were their superiors' personal property and dissolved. The monks took capacities or transferred to other places of religion. According to Professor Woodward, the continued use of the procedure of transfer indicates that as yet the Government had no intention of dissolving all the monasteries. Other scholars, like Dr Parker and Professor Elton, would disagree. Parker says that an alarmed Government, both out of revenge and in order to remove as quickly as possible anything another rebellion could try to defend, had already decided to put an end to the religious houses. Elton feels that despite the kind words in the 1536 Act the suppression of the greater houses had always been intended. But he says that the collapse of the rising, which he calls 'their last hope', encouraged them to make a free surrender of themselves and their property to the Crown.

Furness in Lancashire was the first abbey to make such a surrender. Some of the monks had verbally supported the rebel cause, but there was no good excuse for charging the Abbot with treason and confiscating his house. Thus it was suggested to him that he should give up his abbey of his own free will. He did so, and again precedent was followed and the monks given the right of transfer.

The surrender of the greater houses

It was probably late in 1537, according to Woodward, that the Government at last decided to make total dissolution its aim. In November and December four south-country monasteries surrendered, the first – Lewes – in similar circumstances to Furness. The Prior, being in danger of having a treason charge preferred against him, decided that surrender and a pension was the lesser of two evils. Other houses followed suit in January. By now the new theological ideas were deep-rooted at court, and the moral case against the monasteries had been replaced by a criticism of their religious duties as 'dumb ceremonies'. As Woodward points out, no attempt at reformation could answer this. Total abolition was the only answer. Further indication of the Government's intention can be deduced from the fact that monks and nuns were no longer given the option of moving to other houses of their orders. They were all retired on pension.

People were quick to realize that universal suppression was intended and abbots began to make more leases than ever before. The right to present to vicarages was similarly doled out to friends who would remember the monks when vacancies occurred. Plate and other moveable assets were converted into cash. To prevent this state of affairs from continuing, Cromwell wrote to the heads of surving houses to tell them that all recent surrenders had been voluntary and that a general suppression was not planned. There was also a veiled threat of trouble if alienations continued. It had the desired effect.

In 1538 another royal commission set out to visit all remaining houses, offering a prepared form of surrender and promise of fair reward. Reluctance to sign would only have meant a poorer pension or worse, so usually the commissioners met with success, though sometimes only after prolonged negotiation.

On 6 February 1538 Richard Ingworth, ex-Provincial of the Dominicans and suffragan Bishop of Dover, set out to visit his brethren, the mendicant friars. He gave them the choice of surrendering their houses and entering the secular world, or staying in their houses and following injunctions he would give them, forcing them to a far stricter adherence to the rules of their orders than ever before. They chose the former alternative, and by March 1539 there were no friars left in England.

Meanwhile there had been resistance from two of the monasteries. These were the Priory of Lenton and the Abbey of Woburn which were not surrendered but passed into royal hands by forfeiture after the condemnation of their heads. In the autumn of 1539 the abbeys of Colchester, Reading and Glastonbury fell in a similar way. The Abbot of Glastonbury was accused of robbing his abbey of its treasures; the others died for treasons, the details of which are somewhat obscure. An important element in the case against them was their reluctance to surrender their abbeys. Although denial of the King's supremacy was mentioned at the trials of the Abbots of Woburn and Reading, the main cause of disaffection was probably once again the desire to keep what was treasured. The Abbot of Colchester claimed that the efforts made to get him to surrender his house were illegal, that the King could not by law suppress any house of religion worth more than £200 a year. To legalize the surrenders which had taken place and those that might yet occur,

Parliament passed what is usually called 'the Second Dissolution Act' of 1539.

In November 1539 a team of commissioners, headed by Walter Hendle, Solicitor of the Court of Augmentations, and including Drs Legh and Layton, set off for the North of England with definite instructions to suppress or alter all remaining religious houses. Alteration meant the conversion of an existing monastic cathedral chapter into a secular one, or the conversion of a monastery into a cathedral or collegiate church. The fate of the reluctant abbots seems to have persuaded their brethren against any resistance they might have contemplated. Waltham Abbey, Essex was England's last surviving religious house. It surrendered on 23 March 1540.

Profit to the Crown

One popular misconception about the dissolution of the monasteries which has been a long time a-dying is the belief that once the Crown got the monastic lands into its possession it proceeded to give them away in order to win support for its religious policy. Now it is true that some of the men who helped carry out the dissolution – Cromwell himself and the Chancellor and officers of the Court of Augmentations – were rewarded with gifts, and that some courtiers were similarly enriched, but in general, lands were sold or let out at current market prices. Indeed, of 1,593 grants made in Henry's reign, only 41 were gifts, while 28 were combinations of gift with sale or exchange. The Crown aimed to make money out of the dissolution, and make money it did. It had no need to win friends. The break with Rome had been accomplished and accepted before the monasteries began to fall.

Those who bought monastic property were often already landed people who sought to extend or consolidate their estates, sometimes the monastic stewards and bailiffs. Others who knew exactly what they were buying were ex-*Valor* commissioners, and men like Sir Thomas Arundell, Receiver of Augmentations in the South-West, who made extensive purchases in Cornwall,

Wiltshire, Somerset and Dorset, and Sir Leonard Beckwith, who held a similar position in Yorkshire. Some purchasers were already lessees of monastic property before the dissolution; others, though not many, were well-to-do lawyers and merchants out to establish landed families. Yet others may have been speculators, for they soon resold what they had bought, sometimes after having formed a syndicate to make the initial purchase. Dr Woodward thinks it likely they were agents acting for provincial clients who wanted to be spared the trouble and expense of a journey to London. What it is important to realize is that there was no great revolutionary rise of a new landowning class. In some places the change from monastic to lay landlord may hardly have been noticed, for the same people received the rents.

Sales began in December 1539 when a commission was issued to Cromwell and Sir Richard Rich, the Chancellor of Augmentations, to sell lands to a clear yearly value of £6,000. However, little land was alienated during Cromwell's time, and it was only after the most costly of Henry's wars, that with France and Scotland, began in 1542 that most of the lands were sold. The years 1543–7 saw the sale of two-thirds of all the ex-monastic estates, the usual purchase price being twenty times the annual rent. It seems likely that Cromwell had originally intended that only leases should be made, so that the Crown would be assured of a regular income and be independent of parliamentary grants, but the continuation of such a situation was impossible when an impoverished Government was faced with a war which eventually cost perhaps £2 million, more than eleven times the *Valor* assessment of monastic wealth. When the war was over, the Crown was once more on the verge of bankruptcy. The profits of the dissolution had been squandered.

The fate of the monks

It is surprising how many people still have the idea that when the monasteries were dissolved the monks were all turned out without a penny in their pocket to beg for their living. As we have seen, this was not the case. Those who had taken capacities in 1536, and the friars, too, were not given pensions. The latter had always lived off charity, and could, the Government thought, do so in the future. However, there were jobs for them to go to in the Church as chantry priests and stipendiary curates, and outside it as clerical workers, and it is improbable that many starved.

So that they did not fall below their accustomed status, the heads of houses were given pensions, usually, though not always in proportion to the value of their monasteries. The Abbot of Tavistock got £100 a year, the Prioress of Nunburnholme only £3.33. As for the rank and file, those who had held positions of responsibility as sub-priors, bursars, etc., got more than did those who had not, long-serving monks more than novices. To ensure a profit to the Crown from every confiscated property, inmates of smaller houses generally got less than inmates of bigger ones. The minimum for a professed monk was usually £5 a year, somewhere about subsistence level in 1539, but less than that as the years passed by and inflation forced prices up. Then the officials responsible for paying the pensions took their cut, for that was how they got their living, and sometimes payment got into arrears because of the Government's financial troubles. This caused some to sell their pension rights, preferring ready cash to an uncertain annuity.

Many monks supplemented their pensions by taking parochial livings, though taking a Crown one of equal value to a pension meant the forfeiture of the latter. Some monks got a living almost directly on dissolution because of the way monastic rights of patronage had been disposed of in the years just before the suppression. Some of the abbots and priors may already have been in possession of a living when the dissolution took place. Apparently the Abbot of Torre had become Vicar of Townstall, a Torre living, in July 1531, and he seems to have retained it with his pension of £66.67 until his death in 1556. In general however, the evidence in the bishops' registers seems to indicate that many ex-monks had a long time to wait before they got parishes, for there were a large number of secular clergymen serving as curates, stipendiary priests and chantry priests with a prior claim to be presented to vacant livings. Some of the ex-monks were of course too old or infirm to take any sort of employment, but here the Government usually showed compassion. Richard Lewis, a canon of Bodmin, who was a hundred years old and blind, received the comparatively large sum of £10 and six dozen 'woods' yearly. In view of the recipient's age, this pension was not to be paid for very long, but some pensioners, like the monk of Pershore who died as Rector of Dauntsey, Wiltshire in 1601, proved a little more costly to maintain.

The dissolution of the monasteries had the effect of reducing the number of candidates for ordination, for not only did a large body of extra clergy enter the employment market, monks no longer came forward for ordination, and a very popular source of titles for secular priests had gone. In the diocese of Exeter, between 20 September 1539 and 29 March 1545 only 30 men were ordained priests. In 1534 61 candidates had been so ordained The ordination of 29 March 1545, at which only 1 man was priested, was the first to be held for a year and there were no more until 1551.

It had been the King's plan to turn 13 monasteries into cathedrals of new dioceses. This did not happen in fact. There were other more pressing calls on the newly acquired wealth, such as the need to strengthen coastal defences. However, 6 new sees were created, those of Bristol, Chester, Gloucester, Oxford, Peterborough and Westminster, the last of which was only to survive till 1550. The monastic chapters of Canterbury, Carlisle, Durham, Ely, Norwich, Rochester, Worcester and Winchester were abolished and replaced by secular chapters, sometimes with the same members as before and in seven out of eight cases headed by a dean who had previously served as prior. These cathedrals and the new ones became known as Cathedrals of the New Foundation.

If some abbots and priors became deans, other religious were luckier still and became bishops. The character of the episcopate began to change as ex-monks and friars with a theological education replaced the secular civil-lawyers on the episcopal bench in the House of Lords, a body which, of course, no longer had heads of religious houses among its members. It is noteworthy that the higher clergy, who, though once a majority, were now a minority of the Lords, now began to play a smaller and smaller part in the field of government. The nationalized Church provided fewer government servants than the un-nationalized one; top administrative jobs now tended to go to laymen.

At Peterborough it was the last abbot who became the first bishop. At Oxford, the Abbot of Osney became a bishop when his church was given cathedral status. The Abbot of Tewkesbury became the first Bishop of Gloucester. In time the Master of Sempringham became Bishop of Lincoln and then Archbishop of York, the Prior of Worcester became Bishop of Lincoln, and the Prior of Sheen, Bishop of Man. Heads of religious houses had long held positions as bishops *in partibus*. Now that the Church had been nationalized they took English titles and became suffragan bishops of places like Berwick, Shaftesbury and Shrewsbury.

A quite large number of ex-friars became bishops. Most of them were men of the New Learning, and some played an important part in the ecclesiastical revolution which was taking place. For example, the Dominicans provided John Scory, bishop successively of Rochester, Chichester and Hereford, John Hilsey, Bishop of Rochester, and Richard Ingworth, suffragan Bishop of Dover on the radical side; and Drs Griffith and Hopton, Bishops of Rochester and Norwich respectively, on the conservative.

Other results of the dissolution

How disastrous was the dissolution? The ruins of monastic buildings give some indication of the architectural treasures which were lost. But one should not forget the ones which were saved – usually those churches which had served not only the monks but also the local lay community, who sometimes bought them so that they would continue to function as their parish churches. Thus we still have great minsters like those at Selby and Tewkesbury, which rival cathedrals in their grandeur, and magnificent naves like those at Lanercost, Bolton and Shrewsbury, reminding us that the now ruined or vanished chancel was the monks' church, the nave the laity's. Their furnishings were taken away, of course, and one can only regret the destruction of so many priceless art treasures to fill the Crown's coffers to the tune of some £75,000 and to prevent idolatry. The destruction of the monastic libraries must also be a matter for great regret, though the King did make an effort to make sure that the choice items were salvaged for his own collection.

Their buildings unroofed for the highly prized lead, many monastic sites became stone quarries which were sometimes used by the new estate owners as a source of materials with which to build their mansion houses. It is perhaps some compensation for the loss of the religious buildings that places like Fountains Hall, Woburn, Stoneleigh and Nostell rose immediately or eventually on or near their sites.

In the past much has been written by way of criticism of the new landlords. They have been portrayed as the very opposite of the charitable monks – rack-renters who had no intention of continuing the tradition of monastic hospitality. There is, however, no evidence that the laymen were any worse landlords than the religious. They have been blamed with pauperizing their rural population by enclosing land for sheep rearing which required less labour than arable farming; but, in fact, most sixteenth-century enclosure actually took place before the dissolution, and the monks had a part in it and share the responsibility for the rural depopulation which resulted from it. It is true that rents rose quickly after the transfer of the monastic estates to lay ownership, but then so did prices generally, and it is more than likely that the monks, who were realistic rather than ideal landlords, would have raised their rents to keep pace with the increasing cost of living had they kept their properties. Nor were the new landlords necessarily less hospitable than the monks had been. All persons of substance, ecclesiastical and lay, had been expected to entertain travellers in the past, and many laymen had taken a pride in their hospitality. Rising costs, however, led to a general decline in hospitality in the sixteenth century and again, had the monks survived, this would probably have been as noticeable in their houses as in those of the gentry. As it was, the hospitality the monks had offered had probably been regarded by most of them as a commercial enterprise. Many of the monasteries had not entertained travellers within their own walls, but in separate inns, and they had expected their visitors to make a generous contribution towards their funds in return. However, it is undeniable that the loss of the monasteries did cause a great deal of inconvenience in the remoter parts of the country.

Something else the dissolution put an end to was monastic charity, and this has been blamed to a considerable degree for the widespread poverty in mid-sixteenth-century England. The causes of distress were immensely complex and included a rising population and the influx of silver from the New World, but the loss of monastic charity should not be classed as one of them. The amount of charity dispensed may in any case have been negligible. If we take the *Valor Ecclesiasticus* as a guide, we find that the average proportion of a house's income dispensed in this way was $2\frac{1}{2}$ per cent. At Syon Abbey it was as little as 0.3 per cent. However, these figures only represent those charitable acts the religious were legally bound to undertake. They may in fact have given away rather more than they seem to indicate. Every monastery was supposed to give its left-overs from meals to the local paupers, but we lack evidence as to how far this was done and how much it was welcomed. When alms were given they had usually been ordained by the monastery's founder and later benefactors, and the monks were under a legal obligation to dispense them. At Bodmin in Cornwall, for instance, a shilling was distributed amongst the local poor once a week in obedience to the will of the founder.

Some of the people who received monastic charity were not necessarily poor. The King was entitled to grant annuities of a sort, called corrodies, to old servants, who were allotted rooms in monastic houses and often lived in great comfort. In April 1527, John Amadas, an ex-Yeoman of the Guard, became a corrodian of Tavistock Abbey. He was to have two meals and three bottles of ale or three silver halfpennies every day, and a furred robe or, if he preferred it, £1 at Christmas, a chamber for himself with food and candles, and a stable and hay for his horse. Sometimes private persons bought their own corrodies as an insurance against old age, and it is difficult to distinguish in the records between true recipients of monastic charity and such annuitants as these, whose income was guaranteed by the Government after the dissolution.

Even if monastic charity disappeared with the fall of the monasteries, it does not mean that almsgiving ceased. The charity the monks had dispensed had been ordained by laymen, and laymen continued to endow charities, just as they revivified some of the hospitals for the sick the monks had run.

Another cause of poverty, according to the monks' apologists, was the loss of livelihood by thousands of monastic servants. No doubt some of them joined the ranks of the unemployed, but many, particularly agricultural workers, must have been retained by the purchasers of monastic property. The domestic staff would be more likely to suffer than the rest, but where a mansion house was built on the site of a monastery, perhaps they too kept their jobs. In any case, when the monasteries were dissolved, domestics were given a quarter's wages to tide them over till they found fresh work.

It was long the popular belief that the dissolution led to a great decline in English education, but this has not been conclusively proved. The teaching which went on in monasteries was generally either the teaching of novices or else of choristers. Some took in the children of the gentry, for it was customary in the Middle Ages for noblemen and gentlemen to send their sons to be brought up in the households of great men, ecclesiastical and lay, and for those sons to do personal service for their patrons. The tradition continued, of course, after the dissolution. Sometimes schoolmasters were hired to teach the young gentlemen, but the monks rarely, if ever did any teaching themselves, and there is very little evidence of monasteries running schools for local children, although this seems to have happened at Furness and Whalley. Sometimes, as at Sherbourne, they provided scholarships to the local grammar school, and the religious orders maintained houses of study for their members at Oxford and Cambridge, but the overall contribution the monks made to English education was not apparently very great, and the dissolution was probably not the great disaster it has been said to have been. The sixteenth century was notable for the endowment of grammar schools, many of them being founded by people who had gained monastic property at the dissolution. The grammar schools of the old monastic cathedrals were re-endowed, and new cathedral schools were set up at Bristol, Chester, Gloucester, Peterborough and Westminster. The King also used his new wealth to establish five Regius Professorships at each university and to complete, albeit on a smaller scale than originally intended, Wolsey's scheme at Christ Church, Oxford and found Trinity College, Cambridge.

What then were the most regrettable consequences of the dissolution? Some have said that the dissolution was regrettable because it marked the end of the production of great works of art by monks and of their manuscripts, but by now monks had their books written for them by private scriveners and at least one monastery had a printing press. And they bought their works of art from church furnishers in London!

Perhaps the thing most regretted at the time of the dissolution was the end put to the monk's services, carelessly performed though they often were. Their houses had been founded so that prayers might be said for the souls of their founders and their heirs, and in a still religious society they must have counted for much. The workers in the fields and at their looms, the gentry at their cards and at their hunting knew that while they went about their daily tasks and pleasures their souls were benefiting from the sacrifices of praise and thanksgiving being offered up in the hundreds of religious houses throughout the land. When the last monasteries were surrendering to the Crown in 1539 a Lincolnshire correspondent informed Cromwell that he thought

the abbeys are now nothing pitied, the commons perceiving more conveniences to grow from their suppression. Saving that they lose their prayers.

[7] FAITH AND ORDER

The National Church

In the story of the dissolution of the monasteries we can see reflected some important changes in the official attitude towards religion. In 1536 the case for dissolution was the need for reform of morals; in 1539 it was the uselessness of ceremonies, suggesting that the value of prayer for the departed was in doubt. And, when the great monasteries fell, so did the shrines of which they were the guardians. The name of St Thomas Becket, the upholder of the Church's rights against the Crown, was removed from the Calendar, his body from its grave, and the treasures which adorned his tomb were carted off to London. The State's attitude to St Thomas is easy to explain in political terms; the destruction of the shrine of Our Lady of Walsingham can only be put down to greed and/or doubt about the value of pilgrimages and the efficacy of prayer to the saints.

Then there was the promotion of ex-friars, priors and abbots to the episcopal bench, helping to bring about a change in its character. There were other theologians on the bench too – men with firm leanings towards Lutheranism, like Nicholas Shaxton, Bishop of Salisbury, Hugh Latimer, Bishop of Worcester and Edward Fox, Bishop of Hereford, and, heading them all in the King's affections, Thomas Cranmer, Archbishop of Canterbury. However, there were still more conservative bishops with the ear of the King. Chief of these was a proud prelate of the traditional sort – Stephen Gardiner, Bishop of Winchester, the staunchest upholder of the Royal Supremacy.

The Royal Supremacy is the key to all the apparent contradictions in the English Church of the 1530s and 1540s – a Church which still offered Christ in the Mass for the sins of the world, but seemed to doubt the doctrine of Purgatory; a Church which taught the necessity of the mediation of a priest, but which, by providing an open Bible, gave the layman direct contact with the voice of God; a Church with a Latin liturgy and English Scriptures. Two parties with rival theological views were drawn together by their acknowledgment of the King's Supremacy, by an ecclesiastical nationalism, and it was the King's intention to keep them together. In 1545 he made a famous speech to Parliament.

What love and charity is there among you when one calleth another heretic and anabaptist, and he calleth him again papist, hypocrite and Pharisee? . . . I hear daily that you of the clergy preach one against another, without charity or discretion . . . Yet the temporalty be not clear and unspotted of malice and envy. For you rail on bishops, speak slanderously of priests, and rebuke and taunt preachers, both contrary to good order and Christian fraternity . . . Be not judges of yourselves of your fantastical opinions and vain expositions. . . . Be in charity with one another like brother and brother.

Henry was above all anxious for unity among his people, for to the Tudors unity was the prerequisite of peace. But how could there be unity in a state where some believed in justification by faith, others in the efficacy of good works; some that the Mass was a sacrifice of Christ, others that it was a memorial of the Last Supper; some that the consecrated bread and wine of the Eucharist was Christ's Body and Blood, others that it was still simply wheat flour and grape juice; some in auricular confession and priestly absolution, others in the priesthood of all believers? If Henry wanted to hold a people of diverse beliefs together he might have attempted to please as many of them as he could. Some scholars, such as Professor Dickens and Professor Bindoff, believe that he deliberately sought to tread a *via media*, a middle way between superstitious papalism and the Protestant extremism of the Continent. If such a way was followed, its route was by no means straight. There were diversions to left and right caused by the needs of foreign policy, by Cromwell's leanings towards Lutheranism, and by Henry's own dabblings in theology. The result was not less diversity of opinion, but more. At least some of the responsibility for the situation Henry lamented in his speech of 1545 was the Crown's.

Henry and the Lutherans

In 1534 there seemed to be some possibility of the Emperor Charles V, who had been enraged by his aunt's 'divorce', burying the hatchet with Francis of France and joining him in a crusade to bring England back into the Roman fold. Cromwell aimed to keep the Emperor occupied in Germany by allying with his enemies, the Schmalkaldic League of Lutheran princes. After preliminary negotiations conducted by Robert Barnes, the English Lutheran, the princes said they would accept Henry as a member of their League on condition that he gave them financial backing and accepted the statement of Protestant doctrine called the Confession of Augsburg. This Henry would not do. He said that he was capable of deciding what was true Christian doctrine without foreign help, and that was what he did. The search for Lutheran allies did not cease, but for the time being at least Henry seemed to lack enthusiasm for it. Apparently he did not think a Franco–Spanish attack likely.

Articles and injunctions

In 1536 the Church of England produced its first independent statement of doctrine. To some it has seemed an attempt to appease the Lutherans, to others an attempt at compromise typical of a *via media*. Mr Crosse claims that its purpose was to reassure the orthodox that the renunciation of papal authority did not involve any falling away from Catholic doctrine, and to check the excesses of Protestant extremists. Dr Parker and Professor Scarisbrick claim that it was obviously affected by the Wittenberg Articles of the same year, in which the Lutherans had gone as far as they could in conciliating the traditional out-look of the English. Yet Cardinal Pole said that he found in it 'nothing much at variance with Catholic standards'. The English Church has always had a talent for producing ambiguous state-ments. The Ten Articles was one of these. They were officially stated to have been 'devised by the King's highness's majesty to establish Christian quietness and unity'.

Starting with an assertion of the Royal Supremacy, the Articles also asserted the necessity of the Creeds and of the Sacraments of Baptism, Penance and the Eucharist. Perhaps this was a concession to the Lutherans, but the other four traditional sacraments were not denied. The saints were to be honoured but 'not with that confidence and honour which are only due unto God'. The dead were to be prayed for, but without the use of the word Purgatory, which implied the doctrine of indulgences, for 'the place where they be, the name thereof, and the kind of pains there . . . be to us uncertain by Scripture'. The phraseology concerning the Real Presence of Christ in the Sacrament of the Altar could be interpreted as implying either Catholic transubstantiation or Lutheran consubstantiation. On the important subject of justification, Luther's disciple Melancthon was referred to, but, perhaps due to Henry's personal feelings on the matter, good works as well as faith were then declared to be necessary for salvation.

In the month following the publication of the articles, the first state injunctions for the secular clergy were issued. Designed to raise the standard of teaching and conduct among the priesthood, they followed the traditional pattern of the injunctions of the Universal Church. However, the clergy were ordered to explain the Ten Articles to their congregations and to preach against the Pope and superstitious practices. They were also to teach their adult parishioners and their children the Lord's Prayer, the Creed and the Ten Commandments in English. A concern for education typical of the age was shown, as well as some anxiety for economic and social stability. Priests were to urge their people to educate their children or apprentice them to honest occupations, since crime and social disorder would otherwise result. Rich clergy were to support scholars at the universities and grammar schools. If non-resident, they were to give at least a fortieth part of their income to the poor and a fifth for the maintenance of the chancels of their churches. So that they would set a good example to their parishioners, they were not to frequent alehouses or spend too much time playing cards and other games, but to occupy their leisure time in studying the Scriptures or some other spiritually profitable exercise, 'having always in mind that they ought to excel all other in purity of life, and should be example to all other to live well and Christianly'.

The Bishops' Book

Doubtless the King approved the Injunctions as a step in the
right direction, but perhaps he had some reservations about
the Ten Articles, reservations which would be played upon by the
conservatives among the episcopate, who must have regarded the
lack of a reference to four of the sacraments in the Articles as a
grave omission. In 1537 Convocation drew up the *Institution of a
Christian Man*, commonly called the *Bishops' Book*. Commended
by Henry for study by the parish clergy, it was an exposition
of the Creed, the Ten Commandments, the Lord's Prayer, the
Hail Mary, and all Seven Sacraments. Yet it did not deny
Lutheran beliefs; it did not impose transubstantiation, and it
emphasized scriptural authority, acknowledging the four missing
sacraments of 1536 as being of less importance than the other
three which had been instituted by Christ himself. More important perhaps, in the section on the Creed it defined the position
of the Church of England in relation to the rest of Christendom.
The Catholic Church was, it claimed, composed of free and equal
national churches.

The Head of the national Church of England was not too well
pleased by the Bishops' Book. At the time of its preparation he
had been concerned only for his third and well-loved wife Jane
Seymour and the approaching birth of her child – the long-
awaited son and heir. When the boy Edward had been born he
gave some time to an examination of the book, and expressed
his disapproval of the author's view of the relative importance of
the various sacraments. To the three major ones he wished to
add that with which he had so much to do, Matrimony. And he
did not agree with what the book said of Confirmation – that it
enabled a Christian to 'attain increase and abundance of the
other virtues and graces of the Holy Ghost' not conferred by
Baptism. He claimed that it merely restored the gifts of sacraments already received. Then he disapproved of the adjective
'holy' being applied to the sacrament of Orders. He did not
apparently want his servants the clergy to be regarded as men
apart. Where the Bishops' Book said that Christ had empowered

the Apostles to nominate their successors, the bishops and priests, he added in the margin, 'Note that there were no kings Christian under whom they did dwell'. It appears that Henry had changed his position radically from that which he had held at the time of the publication of his famous book against Luther. The Bishops' Book made nothing of the prime function of the sacrificial priesthood – the offering of Christ in the Mass; their primary function as far as the authors of the book were concerned was the preaching of the Word – the main task of a Protestant minister. The administration of the sacraments took a second place and the Mass was mentioned only twice in the whole book, and then only in passing. Moreover no distinction was made between the office of bishop and that of priest. And Henry did nothing to correct these ideas. Was he himself moving towards a Lutheran position? He was certainly not the orthodox Catholic some writers would have us believe.

The English Bible

In 1537 the national Church was given a Bible in its own tongue. Convocation had asked for one three years earlier, but the version by Tyndale already widely circulating among lay Englishmen was not acceptable on various grounds, notably its unorthodox view of the Church. What to the hierarchy meant 'priest' was translated by Tyndale as 'elder', and 'church' was 'congregation'. Not only that; some of the textual notes were highly provocative. We have seen what efforts the bishops made to prevent Tyndale's works from circulating in the 1520s. The attitude of most of them had not changed; they wanted a version of the Scriptures translated by orthodox scholars. What they got was a combination of the work of Tyndale and that of Miles Coverdale, an ex-friar who had migrated to the Netherlands and whose work lives on in the version of the psalms in the *Book of Common Prayer*. It had first been published in 1535 as Matthew's Bible, Matthew being the pseudonym of its editor John Rogers. Cromwell and Cranmer persuaded the King that the reading of the Bible under the clergy's supervision was preferable to the unchecked private reading of a faulty translation which was bound to increase if an official Bible were not provided for supervised perusal. Permission was granted for the publication of the hitherto unlicensed Matthew's Bible in 1537, and Coverdale's revision of it, called the Great Bible, was the subject of one of a new set of injunctions issued in 1538. This ordered each Incumbent to provide

one book of the whole Bible of the largest volume in English, and the same set up in some convenient place within the said church that you have cure of, whereas your parishioners may most commodiously resort to the same and read it . . . admonishing them nevertheless to avoid all contention and altercation therein.

This was a forlorn hope. Contention and altercation were more in evidence than ever before, now that everyone could read the Bible in church and interpret it in his own way.

More injunctions

Not only did the new injunctions give the English Church a Bible, they gave its clergy a new duty. They had to provide a register 'wherein ye shall write the day and year of every wedding, christening and burying made within your parish'. In fact, some time before the order went out some parish priests had begun to keep registers of this sort – perhaps to prevent marriages taking place within the prohibited degrees of affinity, which were many more then than now.

Other injunctions in this new series called for the examination of parishioners in the Articles of the Faith and the provision by non-resident incumbents of curates to do their work. Important as these were, far more so was the injunction which ordered quarterly sermons based upon the Scriptures, in which the people were exhorted

not to repose their trust or affiance in any other works devised by men's fantasies beside Scripture; as in wandering to pilgrimages, offering of money, candles and tapers to images and relics, or kissing or licking the same, saying over a number of beads, not understood or minded on . . .

The English Church was not only to be a nationalized Church but a 'reformed' one, and 'feigned images ... abused with pilgrimages and offerings of anything made thereunto' were to be taken down.

The Six Articles

The left wing seemed to be in the ascendancy. The doctrine and practice of the Church of England was now, more than ever, based on Scripture. The negotiations with the Lutheran princes continued. A delegation of German divines came to England for a conference. The result was agreement on thirteen articles, but no official authority was ever given to them. In the Summer of 1538 and again in January 1539 Charles and Francis met and agreed to make no alliance with Henry but by mutal consent. Then the Lutheran princes themselves came to terms with Charles at the Diet of Frankfurt. There seemed to be a need to take precautions, but now theological debates were abandoned, and Cromwell, continuing negotiations begun in June 1538, concentrated on producing a marriage alliance, not with a member of the League but with the Duke of Cleves, a man with Lutheran connections but not himself of the reformed faith.

There was no longer any need to be conciliatory to the Lutherans in matters of religion, and Henry, worried perhaps by the results of the provision of an open Bible, set up a committee of four conservative and four reforming bishops together with his vice-regent Cromwell to produce a 'devise for the unity in religion'. It was perhaps inevitable that such a committee should produce nothing. The King himself took action, getting his conservative adviser Norfolk to present six articles to Parliament for discussion. The result was the Six Articles Act, an Act opposed by Cranmer in both Lords and Convocation, but one with the King's *imprimatur*. He revised the first draft in his own hand and attended the debate on it in the Lords. Transubstantiation was stated to be true, and Communion in one kind, that is the bread, to be sufficient for laymen. Both ideas were regarded by Protestant theologians as unjustified by Scripture. Clerical celibacy was to continue – something hardly likely to be approved by a married archbishop – and vows of chastity, such as those made by the ex-monks and nuns, were to be kept. Private masses were approved and so was auricular confession. Anyone who denied transubstantiation was to be burnt and his property confiscated, even if he abjured. Denial of the other articles led to the same penalties, though abjuration would only mean imprisonment, and the death sentences could only be pronounced after a second offence. More than five hundred Londoners were immediately indicted, Cranmer sent his wife to live with relatives in Germany, and two reforming bishops, Latimer of Worcester and Shaxton of Salisbury, resigned their sees.

Did the Six Articles signify a retreat along the road away from Lutheranism? Professor Scarisbrick suggests that it only called a temporary halt to progress in its direction. Perhaps Henry felt a firm stand of this sort at this time necessary to ensure the unity he so much desired to see in his realm, and he may have been worried by rumours that a crusade was to be launched against heretical England. Doubtless he did believe in transubstantiation, but there is, as Dr Scarisbrick points out, evidence that more unorthodox views were developing in his fertile mind. For example, when the Lords were debating the Articles, the conservative bishops asked his support for their argument that confession to a priest was necessary by the law of God and he replied that it was not required by reason or God's law. The Articles themselves said it was 'expedient and necessary to be retained and continued, used and frequented in the Church of God'. Expediency and not divine command was the argument for its retention. And the King's reason for insisting on clerical celibacy may not have been a theological one. He was to say, two years later, that unless celibacy were enforced, clergy would build up great strength through family patronage, make livings hereditary, and thereby become an even greater threat to the authority of the Crown. What is more, although private Masses were insisted upon in the Articles, there was no mention of their traditional purpose – to serve as a sacrifice for the benefit of the souls of the departed. The fifth article stated that it is meet and necessary that private masses be continued and admitted in this the King's English Church and Congregation, as whereby good Christian people, ordering themselves accordingly, do receive both godly and goodly consolations and benefits, and it is agreeable also to God's law.

In 1540 certain events took place which suggest that the Six Articles legislation may indeed only have been intended as a temporary measure taken at a time of danger from abroad and disunity at home. The savage Act was amended slightly; priests and women twice convicted of living in sin were not to be executed. In fact only six people suffered under the Act altogether. The five hundred who had been rounded up were released by a general pardon in which Henry forgave his subjects all heresies, treasons, felonies, and many other offences committed before 1 July 1540. There is evidence that the King was already contemplating issuing some new articles of faith, for he required his bishops to answer a questionnaire dealing with seventeen points of faith and order. He examined their replies and made notes on them which reveal something more of his own views on religion. One set of answers said that there was scriptural authority for the laying on of hands in Confirmation. Henry commented that 'laying on of hands being an old ceremony of the Jews is but a small proof of Confirmation'. He was equally critical of the argument put forward for the use of the chrism in the ceremony. He was not convinced that there was scriptural authority for the sacrament at all. He had reservations too about accepting the sacrament of Unction as one scripturally ordained. He had already objected to the traditional view of the sacrament – that it was 'a visible sign of an invisible grace' – when he had found it in the Bishops' Book, despite the fact that his book against Luther had given the same explanation of the ceremony of annointing the sick. Now when an answer to the questionnaire asserted that 'Unction of the sick with prayer is grounded in Scripture', he wrote in the margin, 'then show where'. He also cast doubt on the traditional view that ordination by laying on of hands with prayer and fasting was something instituted by the Apostles. He did not want to think of the bishops of his

Church as men set apart and elevated by the gift of some special apostolic power. One of his comments on the replies to the questionnaires suggests that he might have been contemplating taking for himself *potestas ordinis* to add to the *potestas jurisdictionis* he had already usurped. One of the replies stated that the making of a bishop was in two parts – appointment, which had been by election in the Apostles' time but was now made by princes, and consecrating. To this Henry replied,

Where is this distinction found? Now, since you confess that the Apostles did occupate the one part which now you confess belongeth to princes, how can you prove that ordering is only committed to you bishops?

If Henry did intend issuing some new, more radical articles, they never appeared. Some other events of 1540 made sure of this.

Cromwell's fall

Despite the royal pardon, 1540 saw at least one notable execution – that of Henry's most loyal and able servant, Thomas Cromwell. The Minister had succeeded in arranging a marriage between Henry and Anne, the Duke of Cleves's sister. Henry agreed to the match without first seeing his much praised bride, and was sadly disillusioned when a plain and dull woman arrived in England. The marriage took place in January; in July it was over – annulled by Convocation, chiefly on the ground of the King's 'defective intention'. Irritated by the humiliation of the match, the continual pressure of the Lutherans to get him to change his Church's doctrine to theirs, and the recent failure of negotiations to gain their alliance, Henry listened to Gardiner and Norfolk – Cromwell's enemies on grounds of jealousy and ambition – when they blamed these things on the Minister. He was attainted of extremely radical heresies and treasons which he had not committed, and on 28 July beheaded.

Two days later a mass execution took place at Smithfield. Three Lutherans, including the famous Robert Barnes, were burned for offences against the Six Articles Act and three

Papists hanged for traitorously denying the Royal Supremacy. Was the King making an example of these people in order to persuade his subjects to follow a *via media* of his own devising, or was there something more to the affair? Professor Scarisbrick believes there was. He thinks that Barnes and possibly the other Protestants were accused not of Lutheranism but of being adherents of one of the extreme Anabaptist sects which had ideas diametrically opposed to Henry's, denying the right of the civil authority to decide religious matters, to compel them to take oaths or to make them bear arms. They were quite certainly innocent of this charge, but they were Cromwell's associates and Barnes was Gardiner's personal enemy, so there was every reason for the conservative faction to want to be rid of them. What better way was there of bringing about their destruction than suggesting that they were, along with the Minister, involved in a dangerous heretical plot? Why did the other victims of 30 July perish? Well, others had died for denying the Royal Supremacy, so there was nothing particularly extraordinary about their fate. That their execution took place when it did was probably because it was a most opportune moment to say 'So perish all traitors'.

The King's Book

With the conservatives in the ascendancy a new royal marriage took place. On the day of Cromwell's execution Henry married Norfolk's nineteen-year-old niece, Catherine Howard. The match did not last long. In 1542 the Queen was convicted of adultery and beheaded. Catherine's charms had not brought Norfolk and Gardiner all the influence they had hoped for. Cromwell's fall might have gone some way towards slowing down religious change, but it did not stop it altogether. A proclamation in July 1541 abolished the 'many superstitious and childish observations' on St Nicholas's and Holy Innocents' Days when choristers were appointed boy bishops, and preached to and blessed the cathedral congregations. Three months later it was ordered that all shrines should be dismantled and that lights should burn only before the Blessed Sacrament.

Since 1539 private persons had been allowed to have Bibles
in their own homes, and if they were less successful in other
respects the conservatives do seem to have been able to convince
the King of the danger from an open Bible to the unity he so
desperately sought. In 1543 they introduced into Parliament a
bill 'for the Advancement of True Religion'. It condemned 'crafty
false and untrue' translations like Tyndale's, and allowed 'no
woman (unless she be a noble or gentle woman)' and no working-
class man to possess any Bible. Realizing how much he relied on
them for support, Henry did not prevent the gentry and the
middle class from reading the Bible. So the most mobile and
influential section of the community, the people who most
wished to be free from the rigidity of Catholicism with its
economic strictures, were free to read, and develop and propagate
their own particular brand of New Learning. The new law therefore had little effect, and in 1545 the King was moved to tell
Parliament:

I am very sorry to know and hear how irreverently that precious
jewel [the Bible] is disputed, rhymed, sung and jangled in every
alehouse and tavern . . .

and in 1546 he again tried to suppress unauthorized versions.

The Act about the Bible promised a definition of doctrine
which appeared in the form of a revision of the Bishops' Book of
1537. Called *Necessary Erudition and Doctrine for any Christian
Man*, it was 'set forth by the King's Majesty of England' as 'a
true and perfect doctrine for all his people'. Henry himself wrote
the preface and the work became known as the *King's Book*.
Again there is evidence that the King was worried about disunity among his people. In his preface he wrote that there had

entered into some of our people's hearts an inclination to sinister
understanding of Scripture, presumption, arrogancy, carnal liberty,
and contention . . .

and there was a reference to the withdrawal of the Bible from
the common man. The right to decide who should read it must
rest with 'the prince and the policy of the realm', and the prince

had esteemed it sufficient for a great many 'to hear and truly bear away the doctrine of Scripture taught by the preachers'.

As might have been expected the King's Book repudiated the 'pretensed universal primacy' of the Bishop of Rome. The only universal governor of the whole Church was Christ whom all Christians were bound to obey. Next to him they should obey Christian kings and princes, 'which be the heads governing under him of the particular churches'. At the same time the book preached a somewhat anti-Lutheran doctrine, either because of the influence of the conservatives or, as is more likely, because an anti-French treaty had recently been concluded with the Emperor.

Transubstantiation was upheld and no distinction was made between the scriptural and non-scriptural sacraments. What is more, the lay demand for communion in both kinds was described as 'pestiferous and devilish'. Good works as well as faith were again asserted to be necessary for salvation, solifidianism being rejected more clearly than before. However, a definition of the word 'purgatory' was avoided and the good works which led to salvation were defined as

inward spiritual works, motions and desires, as the love and fear of God, godly meditations and thoughts, patience, humility and such like . . . not the superstitious works of men's own invention.

And, although 'consecrating and *offering* the blessed body and blood of Christ' was now counted as one of the duties of a minister, it took second place to preaching the Word. In addition the people were warned not to 'deck images gorgeously'. One is therefore, more inclined to agree with Professor Dickens and Miss Carr, who state that the attitude of the years 1536–8 had not been entirely laid aside, and with Dr Parker, who sees in the Book language which derived ultimately from Luther, than with Professor Elton who claims that the book 'came down entirely on the side of traditional orthodoxy' and that 'those traces of Lutheranism which had penetrated into the Bishops' Book of 1537 had quite disappeared'. The doctrine of the King's Book was neither orthodox Catholicism nor straightforward Lutheranism, but something unique – an Anglicanism which was the product of both conservative and reformed influences on the King's mind and designed to meet the requirements of a particular situation.

An English Liturgy

Despite the moderate tone of some parts of the King's Book, Cranmer and men of his leanings seemed to have lost several points to the conservatives, who now began to plot the Archbishop's destruction. However, he had the King's friendship and under his protection was working on the great project of providing the English Church with an English liturgy. He had probably embarked on his scheme by 1538, during the period of negotiations with the Lutherans and when others, including John Hilsey, the ex-Dominican Bishop of Rochester, were producing prymers for the laity. Cranmer's work was based on a variety of source material including a revised Breviary or office book produced by a Spanish friar called Quignon and a prayer book produced by Johann Bugenhagen, a friend of Luther's, as well as the Uses of York and Sarum.

The Breviary then used in the English Church was very complicated and elaborate; nor was there complete uniformity throughout the realm, different areas having different uses. In 1541 Convocation had made an attempt to produce a revised edition of it, in Latin but purged of all references to the Pope, and of 'other things repugnant to the Christian order of our King.' It was not till 1544 that Cranmer produced the first instalment of his own work. It was the English Litany, the basis of the present Litany in the *Book of Common Prayer*, though prayers to the saints and the petition for deliverance from 'the Bishop of Rome and all his detestable enormities' are now omitted. Incidentally the 1544 version virtually omitted all prayers to the saints, commemorating them along with the patriarchs and prophets, but replacing the invocation of fifty-eight of them with bidding prayers for the Church.

In 1545 the King's Prymer, in the production of which both

Henry and his Archbishop probably had a share, appeared, and schoolmasters were ordered to use it to instruct their pupils 'next after the A.B.C.', all other prymers being outlawed. Unlike the Hilsey version, which had been sponsored by Cromwell, the new book had virtually no commemoration of saints in the Calendar.

Henry's last years

By the time of the publication of the Litany, Protestant counsels were again making headway at Court. Catherine Parr, Henry's sixth and last wife, held a daily Bible class with her ladies in waiting and spent long hours telling the King how he should proceed with the cleansing of the Church. Gardiner tried to have her arrested on a charge of heresy, but Henry, to whom she was a great comfort in a time of considerable physical stress, saved her from her enemies just as he had saved Cranmer. While gentlefolk like Anne Askew, a victim of an attempt to prove the heresy of the Queen and other high-ranking women at Court, and her friend John Lascells perished at the stake for denying transubstantiation, other supporters of reform were protected from persecution by the King's favour. Among them were Henry's brother-in-law, Edward Seymour, Earl of Hertford, and John Dudley, Viscount Lisle, the Lord Admiral. We will see how important a part they were to play in the progress of the English Reformation later.

In 1544 Henry, having at last made his peace with Charles and joined him against England's traditional enemies, the French, had become involved in a military campaign in France which was so costly that it led him to seek a new source of revenue. He found it in the chantries, those chapels where Masses were offered for the souls of their founders and benefactors. An Act of 1545 gave him the right to appropriate them and their property to his own use. A survey was conducted and some, but not many, were actually seized. After what was, although Henry denied it, to some extent an attack on the doctrine of Mass for the dead, a committee consisting of Cranmer and two other bishops, set up to investigate the possibility of further liturgical change, suggested the abolition of such ceremonies as bell ringing on Hallowe'en, the covering of images in Lent, and kneeling to the Cross on Palm Sunday. Henry not only accepted these suggestions but went further. He said there was to be no kneeling to the Cross at any time and decreed that the 'greater abuse' of 'creeping to the Cross' on Good Friday should be immediately abolished. However, these decisions were made after the Emperor had deserted him in the war against France. When, shortly afterwards, news reached him that progress was again being made in negotiations with Charles, he countermanded his order. However, he sent a message to Cranmer telling him not to despair of reform but to 'forbear until we may espy a more apt and convenient time for that purpose'.

1546 was a year of negotiations with foreign powers. In the spring, feelers were once again put out for an alliance with the Lutherans, and a conference of learned men from both sides to draw up a common statement of faith was suggested. Then in June peace was at last concluded with France and in August Henry, so Cranmer tells us, announced an agreement with King Francis in which they had decided

not only within half a year to have changed the mass into a communion ... but also to have utterly extirpated and banished the Bishop of Rome and his usurped power out of both their realms and dominions.

The scheme did not come to fruition. Before the six months were up Henry was dead. Had he lived, would the Mass have been abolished in England at least? It is possible. As we have seen, recent formularies of the Anglican Church had made little of the sacrificial aspect of the clergy's functions, and Cranmer was busy preparing that English *Order of Communion* which was to be the basis of the present Communion Service of the Church of England. Perhaps only political expediency would have prevented what was to happen in his son's reign from happening in Henry's. The English Protestant, John Hooper said in 1546 that if the Emperor lost the war he was then waging with the Schmalkaldic

League, the King of England would 'take up the gospel of Christ', and if he won he would 'retain his mass'.

Was it political expediency or zeal for reform which led him to commit his son's education to men with Protestant leanings, and, when he knew he was dying, to nominate a Council of Regency in which the Protestant element, headed by Seymour and Dudley, was strongest? (Even Bishop Gardiner was omitted – though here the reason could possibly have been a quarrel over some church lands the King had coveted – and Norfolk lost his claim to a share in the government through his son's demands for the Regency for him alone.) Perhaps he believed that only with such a Government would England remain independent of Rome.

The true views of this theological dilettante must remain something of an enigma. It is extremely difficult to tell at any stage how far his later religious policies were motivated by his personal beliefs and inclinations, how far by the need to keep peace at home, and how far by the need for allies against foreign foes. Though we have evidence which suggests that he was moving steadily along the path of reform, can we really be certain that he did not still cling to his belief in transubstantiation and the view that faith without works is dead? He certainly asked for the prayers of the saints in his will at a time when more and more people were omitting such invocations. Of one thing we can be fairly sure – his determination to die Supreme Head of the Church of England. In early August 1546 an emissary had arrived from Rome to say that Pope Paul was willing to approve everything Henry had done, including the 'divorce' and the dissolution of the monasteries, if only he would accept his primacy. The reply was an uncompromising 'No'. It was on the morning of 28 January 1547 that the man whose realm in a very peculiar sense bore witness more than any other to the dictum *cujus regio, ejus religio* forsook his earthly kingdom, his hand gripping Cranmer's to indicate his faith in his Saviour.

Further Reading

What is generally regarded as the classic account of the dissolution of the monasteries can be found in *The Religious Orders in England*, Vol. 3 (Cambridge University Press, 1961) by Professor David Knowles, himself a Benedictine monk. Among shorter works, Geoffrey Baskerville, *English Monks and the Suppression of the Monasteries* (Jonathan Cape Paperbacks, 1965) is very readable. In this book, first published before the War, the author set out to give a truer picture of the life of the religious on the eve of the dissolution than that produced by some previous writers who had tended to be over-sympathetic towards the monks. Perhaps he went too far in the opposite direction. More reliable is G. W. O. Woodward, *Dissolution of the Monasteries* (Blandford Press, 1966), where there are useful transcriptions of original documents such as a bishop's visitation findings, part of the *Valor Ecclesiasticus*, deeds of surrender and Augmentations accounts. The social consequences of the dissolution are discussed at some length in A. G. Dickens, *The English Reformation* (Collins and Fontana, 1967). For a detailed account of the dissolution in a particular area, see G. A. J. Hodgett, 'The Dissolution of the Religious Houses in Lincolnshire' in *Lincolnshire Architectural and Archaeological Society's Reports and Papers*, 4th series, part 1, 1951. For a regional study of the fate of monastic property see Joyce Youings, 'The Terms of the Disposal of the Devon Monastic Lands' in *English Historical Review*, 2nd series, vol. 10, 1958. A good account of the troubles in the North, albeit one with rather limited terms of reference, is Christopher Haigh, *The Last Days of the Lancashire Monasteries and the Pilgrimage of Grace* (Manchester University Press, 1969). A short general account can be found in Anthony Fletcher, *Tudor Rebellions* (Longmans, 1968), which also contains transcriptions of relevant documents. Resistance to Henry's policies is discussed in a new book by Professor Elton, *Policy and Police, The Enforcement of the Reformation in the Age of Thomas Cromwell* (Cambridge University Press, 1972).

For a simple and straightforward account of the history of the English Church in the later years of Henry VIII's reign see Gordon Crosse, *A Short History of the English Reformation* (Mowbrays, 1950); for a more scholarly one, T. M. Parker, *The English Reformation to 1558* (Oxford University Press, 1966). The character of the episcopate in the period is closely examined in Lacey Baldwin Smith, *Tudor*

Prelates and Politics, 1536 to 1558 (Oxford University Press, 1953). Much interesting new light is thrown on the King's views on theological matters in the book by Professor Scarisbrick mentioned on page 70 and in Professor Smith's account of the latter years of his reign, *Henry VIII, the Mask of Royalty* (Jonathan Cape, 1971). Another recent book on the period is M. D. Palmer, *Henry VIII* (Longmans, 1971), where there are useful transcriptions of source material. For the intricacies of foreign policy which it is impossible to deal with in a book of this size and scope see R. B. Wernham, *Before the Armada, the Growth of English Foreign Policy, 1485–1588* (Jonathan Cape, 1966).

Principal Events

1535. *Valor Ecclesiasticus*. Royal visitation of the monasteries
1536. Act for the Dissolution of the Lesser Monasteries. Pilgrimage of Grace. Ten Articles. First Royal Injunctions
1537. *Bishops' Book (Institution of a Christian Man)*
1538. Second Royal Injunctions
1539. The Great Bible. Act for the Dissolution of the Greater Monasteries. Act of Six Articles
1540. Marriage with Anne of Cleves (January). Annulment (July). Cromwell executed
1543. Act for the Advancement of True Religion (limiting the reading of the Bible). *King's Book (A Necessary Doctrine and Erudition for Any Christian Man)*
1544. The English Litany
1545. Act vesting chantry property in the Crown. The King's Prymer
1546. Proposal for turning the Mass into a Communion Service
1547. Henry's death (28 January)

PART IV
The Edwardian Reformation

[8] SOMERSET AND THE DESPOLIATION OF THE CHURCH

The Lord Protector

Henry's heir and successor, Edward VI, was a boy of nine – precocious and priggish, with his father's interest in theology, and, owing to the tendencies of his tutors and guardians, with leanings towards Protestantism which became more and more marked as time went on. He did not, of course, rule the country, but then neither did the Council appointed by his father. Edward's uncle the Earl of Hertford, Jane Seymour's brother, took possession of the boy and persuaded his fellow councillors to give him the Regency and the title Lord Protector.

The dissolution of the chantries

Somerset was both ambitious and greedy and, like so many greedy men in his day, he saw the Church as a source of wealth – wealth to bolster up the sickly finances of the State, and wealth to be used for his personal aggrandizement.

The Act which had provided for the transfer of chantry property to Henry VIII had only been intended to be operative during that King's lifetime. Somerset, who was as much an Erastian as Henry himself – that is, he believed in the thesis later to be propounded by the Swiss theologian Thomas Erastus that the Church should be subordinate to and directed by the secular power – decided that the uncompleted dissolution of the chantry foundations should be continued. And not only were the properties of chantries to be assigned to the Crown, but also those of free chapels, colleges, fraternities, guilds and hospitals. Henry's Act had stated that the confiscation was necessary because of the great cost of the war against France and Scotland. The statute now passed brought into the open the theological argument for dissolution. Parliament, it declared, considered

that a great part of superstition and errors in Christian religion hath been brought into the minds and estimation of men, by reason of the ignorance of their very true and perfect salvation through the death of Jesus Christ, and by devising and phantising vain opinions of purgatory and masses satisfactory, to be done for them which be departed . . .

These errors had been promoted through the use of chantries, but now their funds could be devoted to

the erecting of grammar schools to the education of youth in virtue and godliness, the further augmenting of the Universities, and better provision for the poor and needy.

When, however, commissions were later issued for the sale of chantry lands, it was revealed that the institutions had been dissolved not simply for these reasons but

specially for the relief of the King's Majesty's charges and expenses, which do daily grow and increase by reason of the divers and sundry fortifications, garrisons, levying of men and soldiers.

As a matter of fact, many chantry foundations already provided both for education and for the relief of the poor. Sometimes a chantry priest performed the functions of village schoolmaster in addition to his liturgical duties, and chantry incomes occasionally helped support scholars at the universities. Sometimes too, the poor were helped by monetary payments and gifts of food and clothing. There was considerable opposition to the dissolution in Parliament, but this was largely due to fears that the general funds of secular guilds, which were used for the mutual benefit of members and their dependants, would be seized. When the Government explained that it intended only to levy a charge on the guilds to cover funds hitherto used for 'superstitious' purposes, such as masses for the dead, this opposition was overcome. Actually there was a general falling off of interest in the chantry foundations as such. Donors, founders and others in numerous places were found by the commissioners who surveyed chantry property prior to dissolution to be expelling priests and appropriating chantry revenues to their own use. Perhaps they anticipated that if they did not do so, the Crown would.

Not all the estimated 2,374 chantries, 90 colleges and 110 hospitals disappeared at the dissolution. The commissioners sometimes recommended the preservation of chapels in remote areas to serve as chapels of ease to parish churches, and some, though not all, chantry schools were re-founded as Edward VI Grammar Schools. Moreover, Professor Jordan has calculated that in time confiscated chantry wealth was used to increase the endowments supporting the schools by almost a third, but the promised new schools were slow to appear. Those almshouses and leper hospitals run from chantry endowments and functioning at the time of the dissolution were allowed to continue, and the Chantry commissioners used chantry funds to establish or re-establish thirteen more. The collegiate churches whose staffs performed parochial duties also survived, but sometimes with only one priest instead of several.

The priests who lost their posts joined the ranks of the large but dwindling body of unbeneficed clergy, which included monks who had still not acquired livings (and now the chantries had gone had less chance of doing so), and found themselves curacies or lived off their pensions. Those who had £5 or under from their chantries were awarded pensions equal in value to their former stipends; the others got something between £5 and £6.67, though they might previously have had an annual income of up to £20. However, they were free to seek benefices without loss of pension; indeed the chantry commissioners recommended some priests to the Government as fit men to serve cures, though some must have had a long wait before they got them.

As had happened when the monasteries had been dissolved,

the Crown reserved the bells and lead of the confiscated buildings to its own use. The buildings themselves and the lands which gave the priests their income were sold by the Court of Augmentations. Individual chantry properties were, of course, much smaller than monastic ones, and they were sold as parts of large lots of property, sometimes well-scattered throughout the country. For example, Sir Thomas Bell and Richard Duke, who was Clerk of Augmentations and must have had a good idea of the real value of the property he was investing in, paid £1,297.50 for a lot which included possessions in Devon, Somerset, Gloucester, London and the North Riding. And this was not simply real estate. Thrown in for good measure were some dozen cows which had lately been given to pay for obits in parish churches!

The dissolution seems to have passed off with very little trouble. There was a small uprising in the Ayton district of Yorkshire in which a chantry commissioner and some of his associates were killed. The local chapel had been dissolved, but the troublemakers had more grievances than that. We have no real indication of how many Englishmen really regretted the passing of the chantries, but a good number of them must still have believed that the masses said there had benefited the souls of their departed relatives and have felt the loss.

Secularization of episcopal lands

The story of how Somerset acquired the site for his magnificent palace of Somerset House by demolishing three bishops' town houses and a parish church, and materials for it by destroying the cloister of St Paul's Cathedral and part of the Priory Church of St John of Jerusalem is well known. Not so well known is the way in which he and his fellow Council members robbed the bishops of their episcopal estates. The Protector went even further in his Erastianism than Henry had gone, issuing new commissions to the bishops which made their offices tenable only at the Crown's pleasure and subject to their good behaviour. Any cleric who wanted a bishopric and any bishop who wanted to keep his post had to be prepared to make concessions. Henry

Holbeach, Bishop of Lincoln, who received the temporalities of
his see on 19 August 1547, two days later handed over to Somerset the manors of Thame, Dorchester, Banbury and Woburn.
In 1535 the estates of the Bishop of Exeter had been valued at
£1,441.86. In the years which had followed he had responded
to King Henry's requests and made leases of his manors to such
people as Sir Thomas Darcy and Sir Thomas Speke, Gentlemen
of the Privy Chamber, and Clement Throckmorton, Queen
Catherine Parr's Cupbearer, at rents based on the 1535 valuation,
with the result that his see's income had not kept pace with rises
in property values. Under Somerset he was even less fortunate.
He was asked to hand over his properties to men like the
Protector's secretary, Thomas Fisher, and the Comptroller of
the Household, Sir William Paget as free gifts. In less than two
years he gave away his house in London, fourteen manors and
estates and two boroughs, which in 1535 had been worth £902.53
to his see. Earlier in his episcopate he had granted another manor
worth £32.38 to the Crown. In addition he had granted long-term
leases of all his see's ten other properties apart from his palace
at Exeter, and two other small properties, the three of which had
been worth a mere £170.20 in 1535. The sees of Bristol, Carlisle,
Coventry and Lichfield, Salisbury and Bath and Wells also lost
some of their possessions (the last to provide estates in Somerset
appropriate to the Protector's ducal title) as part of a process of
secularization which had begun under Henry VIII and was to
continue under Somerset's successor, and in which chapter lands
and advowson also changed hands.

[9] LITURGICAL REFORM

Reform legislation

Somerset had long had leanings towards Lutheranism and once
in office established contact with continental reformers, notably
Calvin. He could not, however, be described either as a Lutheran

or a Calvinist, for his views were as much his own as were Henry VIII's. However, he was certainly eager to press on with the reform of the Church.

During the summer of 1547 the powers of the bishops in their dioceses were temporarily suspended while a team of royal commissioners toured the country publishing new injunctions. They ordered each parish to obtain a copy in English of the *Paraphrases* of Erasmus, so that parishioners could read his criticisms of the pomp and covetousness of the Church. Another book each church had to have was the *Book of Homilies*. This was a collection of sermons compiled by Archbishop Cranmer – no doubt a useful volume at a time when few parish clergy were competent preachers. The homilies were not particularly controversial in character, although one on good works contained a lively attack on the old superstitions it was desired to eradicate. Once again each parish was ordered to have an English Bible, and from it were to be read the Epistle and Gospel at High Mass. A new Bidding Prayer was ordered for use in the daily offices. In it, prayer for the dead was still enjoined but only in general terms. Again objects of pilgrimage and idolatry were to be destroyed, whether statues, wall paintings or windows, and a pulpit had to be set up in every church.

The injunctions met with a mixed reception. Bishops Gardiner of Winchester and Bonner of London opposed them. Gardiner, perhaps still smarting after being left out of the Council of Regency, did so on the pretext that they lacked parliamentary sanction and that the Royal Supremacy was in abeyance during the King's minority. Both bishops were committed to the Fleet prison. Bonner soon submitted and gained his release, but Gardiner remained in prison until a general pardon was proclaimed in January 1548. No doubt the injunctions pleased those with Protestant inclinations, especially the iconoclasts, many of them nothing more than hooligans, who had already done irreparable damage in cathedrals and churches up and down the land.

The injunctions were followed by an Act which changed the method of appointing members of the episcopacy, who were now charged to preach in their dioceses at least four times a year.

The elaborate system of *congé d'élire* was abolished. In future bishops were to be appointed by letters patent and to hold their courts in the King's name. More striking was an Act which repealed the harsh additions King Henry had made to the treason laws, as well as the Statute *De Heretico Comburendo*, the Six Articles Act, and restrictions on printing, reading, teaching or expounding the Scriptures. However, yet another Act made reviling the Holy Sacrament, not only in sermons, but in 'rhymes, songs, plays or jests', punishable by fine or imprisonment. It was a most cunningly framed statute, for it also included provision for communicants to receive the Chalice as well as the Host. Conservatives were bound to vote for the Act to put an end to what they considered the blasphemy of those who spoke of the Sacrament as 'Jack in the Box' or 'Round Robin', or mocked the sacred words of consecration, *Hoc est corpus*, as Hocus-pocus. Therefore, radicals, who regarded the restriction of the Chalice to the priest as unscriptural, got their way.

The immigrants

As a land without heresy laws and with virtually complete freedom of speech for the Protestant preacher, England became the Mecca of those unable to find the religious liberty they sought on the Continent, over five thousand poor refugees from France and the Netherlands settling in London alone.

In May 1548 Charles V was in a strong enough position to impose the Interim of Augsburg on the Holy Roman Empire. It was supposed to be a compromise between Protestantism and Catholicism, and indeed went so far as to permit clerical marriage and Communion in both kinds. However, it retained transubstantiation, prayer to the saints and the Seven Sacraments. As a result of the Interim, over four hundred Protestant ministers are said to have left Germany. Those who came to England were largely of one or other of two schools of thought (at that time on the point of uniting on the Continent) – Zwinglian or Calvinist.

Ulrich Zwingli had developed his own brand of Protestantism independently of Luther and had a different view of the significance of the Sacrament. He interpreted the words of institution used by Christ at the Last Supper and by the priest at every Mass, 'This is my body', as meaning 'This signifies my body'. The Holy Communion was for him an act of remembrance. He denied the Real Presence of Christ in the bread and wine, but taught that the communicant received a spiritual grace. Zwingli's tenure of this somewhat complicated idea prevented him from coming to any sort of compromise with Luther who clung tenaciously to his belief in consubstantiation.

The first stronghold of Zwinglianism was the Swiss town of Zürich, where the Reformer had served on the staff of the Great Minster. Zürich was the capital of the most important state in the Swiss Confederation, and other states followed its example in adopting the Faith which Zwingli taught.

John Calvin also lived in a Swiss city – Geneva. By birth, however, he was French. He had left his homeland to avoid persecution and settled first at Strasbourg and then at Basle. There he had published his great thesis on the faith and duties of a Christian, the *Institutes of the Christian Religion*. In it he had expounded the doctrine of Predestination, that

... all are not created in equal condition; rather eternal life is ordained for some, eternal damnation for others.

Calvin did not invent this gloomy doctrine and most thoroughgoing denial of the efficacy of good works; he merely developed it. It had already been outlined in the writings of Martin Luther, who had himself found it in the works of St Paul and St Augustine.

At Geneva, where he had considerable influence over the City Council, Calvin set about organizing a reformed Church. In this Church there was no hierarchy. All pastors were equal, though there was an elected Consistory of six ministers and twelve lay elders to give guidance to the other believers. Sabbath day observance was enforced; gambling, dancing, theatre going, excessive meals and extravagance in dress were all prohibited, and the Council saw to it that offenders were punished. Calvin hoped that Somerset would run England on similar lines but, even if the Protector had wanted this, which is unlikely, it was not a practicable proposition in so big a country. Although Calvin corresponded with a number of influential Englishmen, he probably had little direct influence on English theology in Edward's reign. However, his interpretation of the Sacrament was that which eventually came to be widely accepted in England, that Christ was present in the bread and wine in a spiritual sense.

Perhaps the most influential newcomer to England, and the most interesting, Martin Bucer, was not so much a disciple of Calvin as his mentor, his influence on the 1539 edition of the *Institutes* being quite noticeable. The leader of the reform movement in Strasbourg, when the Interim was imposed on that city he accepted the warm invitation of his admirer, Cranmer (who hoped to bring Protestants of all parties into some sort of unity), and soon became Regius Professor of Divinity at Cambridge. He was a tolerant man, who believed that outside the primary tenets of the Faith there were many points (*adiaphora*, or things indifferent) on which differences of opinion were inevitable and tolerable, a view shared by a kindred spirit, Luther's successor Melancthon. Other former residents of Strasbourg who settled here included Peter Martyr, who obtained the Regius chair at Oxford, and Paul Fagius, who was appointed Reader in Greek at Cambridge. When Fagius died, his place was taken by a Calvinist – John Immanuel Tremellius, who, curiously, had started life as a Jew and had been converted to Christianity by Cardinal Pole. Another Calvinist, Valérand Poullain, became superintendent of a colony of Flemish weavers which Somerset had established in the ruins of Glastonbury Abbey. Foreign Protestants in London were allowed to worship in the Church of the Austin Friars and their superintendent minister was John à Lasco, or Laski, friend of Erasmus, and lately superintendent of the Reformed churches of Zealand. His church was run on Calvinistic lines, with ordained and elected elders to enforce a strict discipline. Other newcomers were Francisco de Encinas, alias Dryander, a Spanish nobleman with Lutheran views and much liturgical knowledge, and Bernardino Ochino, an Italian ex-friar who became a prebendary (canon) of Canterbury and published attacks on both Rome and Geneva.

The first Prayer Book

The amount of influence the immigrants had on the Government's religious policy is hard to assess, but there is no doubt that their ideas added to the ferment taking place in English theological thought, particularly at the universities, where Lutheranism lost its preeminence. Zwinglianism and Calvinism must have had an influence on the theologically minded non-academic too, and thereby created more problems for a Government which was beginning to realize what difficulties must inevitably result from religious freedom. Throughout 1548 one proclamation followed another, bearing witness to the confused state of things. One was intended to check the pronouncement by preachers of such outrageous doctrines as the legality of bigamy. But it was too mild, requiring only prudence and forbearance from those who occupied the pulpits. When it proved ineffective, however, another proclamation inhibited preaching altogether, and the words of the *Homilies* were the only ones heard at sermon time. Irreverence seemed to be on the increase. More proclamations forbade quarrelling and shouting in church and the mobbing of priests. It was also found necessary to issue one directed against the theft of sacred vessels and church furniture, and to make a careful inventory of all church goods to keep a check on further misappropriation. Some people seem to have thought that if they did not take these things the Government would – and not without reason. The Council had decreed the removal not merely of those images which were the objects of superstition but of 'all the images remaining in any church or chapel'. Walls were white-limed; roods and side altars were demolished. It must have seemed only a matter of time before the churches would be stripped completely bare. And in at least one place the result of the anti-image proclamation was violence. The lay farmer of the Archdeaconry of Cornwall was murdered after he had given the people of Helston the news, and at least ten of his several assailants, one of them a priest, were hanged, drawn and quartered.

The Council also began to prune the Church's services, cutting out what was considered to be superstitious or unscriptural – the distribution of candles at Candlemas, the imposition of ashes on Ash Wednesday, the carrying of palms on Palm Sunday, creeping to the Cross on Good Friday, the distribution of the Holy Loaf after Mass in order to emphasize the social character of the worshipping community. What Henry had considered doing but had been prevented by the demands of politics was accomplished by his successor. And the Mass was at last converted into a communion service. The first step towards the introduction of the new service was for Cranmer to send a questionnaire to the bishops to ask their opinion of the Mass and whether they thought it should be celebrated in English. Sir Maurice Powicke expresses the view that it was in order that debates could be held on the Mass that the Six Articles and other heresy laws were repealed, and the fate of Bishop Gardiner does seem to suggest that the new toleration was meant to be enjoyed chiefly by those of a Protestant frame of mind. After giving something other than the required answer when asked for his thoughts on the Sacrament of the Altar, he was ordered not to speak of it in public again, and, failing to obey, was sent to the Tower, where he remained till the end of the reign. The radicals among the bishops willingly agreed to Mass being said in English, but the archconservatives Bonner and Tunstall would only countenance the odd prayer or two in the vernacular. To start with, only a small section of the service was said in English. This was contained in the *Order of Communion*, which made its first appearance at Easter services in 1548. The Latin Mass was said unaltered up to the end of the Canon (the prayer of consecration), and then followed an exhortation to Communion, and English prayers of preparation for Communion which appeared in subsequent prayer books – the General Confession, the Absolution, the Comfortable Words from the Scriptures, and the Prayer of Humble Access. The words of administration were in English too, as was the blessing. It is probable that a complete service had already been prepared by Cranmer and that these extracts from it, based largely on Lutheran sources, were meant as a tentative first step towards the the the introduction of the whole.

The new order was published by a proclamation which exhorted men to receive it

with such obedience and conformity that the King might be encouraged from time to time further to travail for the Reformation, and
setting forth of such godly orders as may be most to God's glory, the
edifying of our subjects, and the advancement of true religion; which
thing we, by the help of God, most earnestly intend to bring to good
effect, wishing all our loving subjects in the meantime to stay and
quiet themselves with our direction, as men content to follow authority, and not enterprising to run afore, and so by their rashness become the greatest hinderers of such things as they more arrogantly
than godly would seem hotly to put forward.

But some men did 'run afore', impatiently producing their own
unauthorized English services. By May, Mass, matins and evensong were being said wholly in English at St Paul's Cathedral
and other London churches, while similar experiments were
taking place at the Chapel Royal with the Government's connivance. Added to the various uses of the Latin rite found up
and down the country, they must have resulted in a discon-
certing lack of uniformity similar to that which one finds in the
Church of England in this present age of liturgical reform. The
great diversity of rites and ceremonies was given as the reason
for the introduction of a new office book entirely in English,
when, early in 1549, an Act of Uniformity was passed by
Parliament. The preface to the *Book of Common Prayer* gave
other grounds for its publication – the more full and orderly
reading of the Scriptures; the omission of 'vain and superstitious'
matters; the use of the English language, enabling the people to
understand the services in which they were taking part.

For the first time in England, all the services required by
priest and people were contained in one book. There was a new
congregational service of Matins which fused the old offices of
Matins and Lauds in the medieval Breviary. A similar service
for the other end of the day – Evensong – was a fusion of Vespers
and Compline. The other services of the Church underwent some
modification. Anointing was omitted at Confirmation, though it
still found a place in Baptism; and the sacrament of Holy Unction

gave way to a service for the visitation of the sick. Confession to a priest was sanctioned, but as a matter for personal choice.

It was, of course, the Mass that mattered. But some would see here a genuine attempt to please several shades of opinion. While bishops like Tunstall of Durham, Bonner of London, Day of Chichester, Skip of Hereford, Thirlby of Westminster, Rugg of Norwich and Heath of Worcester upheld transubstantiation, the Archbishop himself (the compiler of the new book), Goodrich of Ely, Holbeach of Lincoln and Ridley of Rochester believed something else. Exactly what they did believe it is difficult to decide. The eucharistic theology of the Archbishop has been a particular cause of dispute among historians. Some think that for a time he believed in Lutheran consubstantiation; others deny it. Some argue that at the time of the compilation of the Prayer Book he took a Zwinglian view of the Sacrament, regarding the Holy Communion as a simple act of remembrance of Christ's death, others that he believed that Jesus was somehow spiritually present in the bread and wine. There is no room here to examine the arguments each scholar has produced to support his theory, but they make fascinating reading. One cannot help thinking, however, that it is perhaps wrong to attempt to categorize the Archbishop's beliefs. He was an intelligent man, learned not only in the eucharistic theology of his own day but also in that of the Fathers of the Church and of the early Middle Ages, and therefore his ideas were constantly developing in a most complex way. Whatever his true view was, he seems to have hoped that those who used the new Prayer Book would see in the Sacrament what he himself saw, and he was genuinely disappointed when Bishop Gardiner claimed that the phraseology implied transubstantiation. Dr Parker argues that the traditional doctrine was not specifically denied in the Book, not as a result of an ambiguity which Cranmer had always intended, but because of conservative pressure from members of the commission appointed to work on its compilation and to the fears of the Government about the reception the Book would have in a country still predominantly of the old way of thinking. The very title given in it to the main service of the Church, *The Supper of*

the Lord and the Holy Communion, commonly called the Mass
suggests an attempt at compromise between the old and the
new, and the retention of the ancient vestments would seem to
some to hint at caution on the Government's part. The service
was in fact largely a translation of the missal of the Use of Sarum
(Salisbury) with prayers from, among other works, the *Consul-
tatio* of Archbishop Herman of Cologne, a conservative attempt
to combine Catholic and Lutheran uses, which had already
contributed to the *Order of Communion*. Scholars have tended to
emphasize either the traditional or the novel aspects of the new
rite. Mr Rice believes that far from being an attempt to intro-
duce into the services of the English Church in a somewhat
ambiguous way new continental theology, it was an attempt to
return to what was thought to be the purer worship of the
primitive Church, long overlaid with medieval corruptions and
complications, and moreover was essentially Catholic in tone.
Professor Owen Chadwick, however, points out that the principles for reform – services must be understood by the people,
who should be active participants and not just spectators, and
provision should be made for their instruction – were Luther's.
In support of his case he quotes a travelling English merchant
who described the new service as being 'after the manner of
the Nuremberg churches and some of those in Saxony'.

Catholic or Lutheran, in one sense at least the new rite was, as
far as English churchmen were concerned, revolutionary. The
Lutheran rite left out the whole of the traditional Canon of the
Mass. Cranmer retained it in modified form, but omitted some
very significant words before and after consecration:

we most humbly pray and entreat [Thee] to accept and bless these
gifts, these presents, this holy immaculate sacrifice which we offer to
Thee . . . in behalf of Thy holy Catholic Church

and

we . . . offer to Thy excellent Majesty of Thy gifts and bounties, a pure,
a holy, a spotless sacrifice, the Holy Bread of eternal life, and the cup
of everlasting salvation.

The Mass is no longer what it was – the offering of Christ

again for the sins of the world. It is simply a memorial of the death on the Cross of Him

who made there (by his one oblation once offered) a full, perfect, and sufficient sacrifice, oblation and satisfaction, for the sins of the whole world.

No longer does the priest pray God to command that

these things (i.e. the consecrated bread and wine) be carried by the hands of Thy Holy Angel to Thy altar on high, before the sight of Thy Divine Majesty.

Now it is 'our prayers and supplications' which are to be taken thither. The only sacrifice priest and people are making is one 'of praise and thanksgiving'.

Dr Parker claims that the phrase 'this sacrifice of praise and thanksgiving' is ambiguous. It could, he thinks, be understood as meaning that the service was a sacrifice for the purpose of praise and thanksgiving. However, that this ambiguity was intended it is difficult to accept when so much else seems to indicate clearly that the English Parliament, on behalf of the English Church, had rejected the traditional concept of the sacrificial priesthood. Communion was now the most important element in its chief service, and it is obvious that at least some of the clergy recognized the essential difference between the old and the new. Robert Parkyn, the Curate of Adwick-le-Street near Doncaster through nearly thirty years of religious change, commented thus:

And so the holy mass was utterly deposed throughout all this realm of England . . . and in place thereof a communion to be said in English without any elevation of Christ's body and blood under the form of bread and wine, or adoration.

The 1549 Rebellions

Some priests refused to use the new service, even though the penalty for not doing so was the loss of a year's stipend and six months' imprisonment. A second offence meant the loss of all benefices and a year in gaol, and a third, life imprisonment. Any person openly attacking the new Prayer Book or procuring a priest to say other rites was to pay a £10 fine for a first offence and £20 for a second, and to forfeit all his goods for a third.

The reluctance to worship in the new way is not surprising when one considers how the slightest innovation a clergyman makes can even today earn him the hostility of his congregation. Perhaps it was partly as a result of congregational pressure that the situation arose which the Council described in a letter to Bishop Bonner, written in June 1549:

the book so much travailed for, and also sincerely set forth, remaineth in many places of this our realm either not known at all, or not used, or at least if it be used, very seldom, and that in such light and irreverent sort as the people in many places have heard nothing; or if they hear, they neither understand, nor have that spiritual delectation in the same, that to good Christians appertaineth.

In one place where the Book was used the result was armed rebellion. That was Sampford Courtenay in Devonshire, where the Rector, William Harper, once chaplain to Queen Catherine Parr, was forced by his parishioners to say Mass in the old fashion. News of this caused villagers in neighbouring parishes to persuade their priests to do likewise. Attempts by local magistrates to make them obey the law failed.

Meanwhile trouble had broken out in Cornwall, where antipathy towards the Government had been increased by the executions already referred to. A Bodmin squire, Humphrey Arundell, had taken charge of a band of insurgents organized on military lines, advanced across country, forcing the gentry to take refuge in Tremston Castle, and besieged Plymouth. His army moved on to meet the Sampford rebels at Crediton.

What did the rebels want? They did not want the Prayer Book, whose services the Cornishmen likened to 'a Christmas Game', arguing that some of them could not understand English. There was probably something in this, since the diocesan Bishop had given permission for priests to teach children the Lord's Prayer, Hail Mary, Creed and Seven Works of Mercy in Cornish. True they could not understand Latin either but at least it was familiar. They wanted the old rites appropriate to Palm Sunday and other Holy Days to be revived, prayers to be said for the dead at Mass and sermon time, and the destroyed statues replaced. They wanted the Sacrament to hang before the altar in its pyx and 'to be worshipped', and Holy Communion in one kind and at Easter only. They also wanted a celibate priesthood, for the clergy had recently been given legal permission to marry like their immigrant counterparts, though they had been advised that it was 'better for the Estimation of Priests and other Ministers in the Church of God, to live chaste, sole and separate from the Company of Women.' In fact, the insurgents wanted all recent legislation to be repealed and no new laws to be passed until the King came of age at twenty-four, and they wanted the Six Articles Act to be revived to prevent further attacks on the Faith. These demands were conservative, but perhaps not quite so conservative as some people seem to think. Professor Elton says that the insurgents wanted the Papal Supremacy to be restored. Professor Bindoff denies that this was so, and it seems that he may well be right, for there was no mention of the Pope in any of the several sets of articles sent by the rebels to the Government, no wish to turn the clock back more than a dozen years. They did, however, want Cardinal Pole back from Rome to sit on the King's Council, and they also wanted two West-country clerics, Dr Moreman and Dr Crispin, who had been imprisoned in the Tower for preaching against the regligious changes, to be released. Some of their other demands seem reasonable enough. They wanted baptism on weekdays – an important matter for people who believed that those who died unbaptized were damned – and more frequent services of Confirmation. Their leaders showed considerable shrewdness in the reason they gave for their demand that the English Bible be withdrawn – otherwise the clergy shall not of long time confound the heretics.

As was the case with other rebellions of a religious nature, there were also some economic causes of discontent. There had been rumours of taxation on geese and pigs, following a recent imposition on sheep and cloth, and the rebels seem to have had some fear of famine. As Mr Fletcher suggests there also seems to have been something of the nature of class warfare about the insurrection, an aspect ignored by Mrs Rose-Troup, who, early this century, wrote what was to be, despite its partisan nature, the standard work on the Rebellion. She claimed that it was 'evident that the best of the county families of Devon and Cornwall contributed to the ranks of the insurgents'. Now it is true that some gentry were involved. Three members of the Arundell family were implicated, but only one sufficiently to be executed when it was all over. Sir Thomas Pomeroy was in the rebel ranks too, but probably more out of pure bravado than because of any religious convictions, for at the time of the rebellion he was engaged in buying chantry lands from the Crown! Members of the minor landowning families of Coffin, Bury and Winslade were also involved, but far more impressive is the list of those in active opposition to the rebels. It includes such well-known West-country names as Carew, Pollard, Denys, Courtenay, Grenville and Raleigh. The rebel army included the chief burgesses of Torrington, Bodmin and St Ives, but the 'Captains of the Camps' were a tailor, a labourer, a shoemaker and a fisherman. They demanded that a gentleman should have only one servant for each hundred marksworth of land he owned. Thomas Cranmer, who replied to the rebels' demands, dealt with this one very bluntly. He accused the insurgents of intending

to diminish their [the gentry's] strength and to take away their friends, that you might command gentlemen at your pleasures.

The rebels also wanted those who owned monastic and chantry land to give up half of what they had, so that two religious houses could be established in Devon and two in Cornwall. Cranmer's comment was that they not only wanted to take from the King

such land as be annexed unto his crown, and be parcel of the same, but also against all right and reason to take from all other men such lands as they came to by most just title, by gift, by sale, by exchange, or otherwise.

The rebels got nowhere with their demands, though Somerset

was willing to remit the tax on sheep and cloth which they objected to. At first he tried gentle persuasion to get them to go home. Two priests were sent to convince them of the error of their ways and, when they failed, two West-country gentlemen, Sir Peter and Sir Gawen Carew were told to go and listen to their complaints. At length, Lord Russell, the Lord Privy Seal, was ordered to take stricter measures with the obstinate, though even he was to 'bring the people with gentleness . . . to conformity', wherever possible.

After two minor skirmishes at Crediton and Clyst St Mary, 2,000 rebels advanced on Exeter and, when the Mayor, who knew better than they what was the most sensible policy for his city to follow, refused to become an officer in their army, they subjected the provincial capital to a siege. One cannot help but question the motives of those rebels who brought their wives with horses and panniers to hold the riches they intended to take from the city. Those of the people who removed the English Bible, *Paraphrases* of Erasmus and Communion Book from a suburban church were more honourable. The Government having set an example in appropriation, church property was no longer safe. Citizens were conscripted for Exeter's defence, and church plate was sold to pay their wages. A silver and gilt pyx was sold to pay for repairs to a church damaged by the rebels, and elsewhere in Devon both plate and vestments were disposed of to help provide Russell with troops to raise the siege.

Exeter was without normal contact with the outside world for six weeks. Then Russell with long-awaited reinforcements defeated advance parties of the rebels at Fenny Bridges, Woodbury Common and Clyst Heath, and relieved the city. After the victory came reward and retribution. The City Council was given a valuable grant of land; the rebels who had attempted to reform their ranks at Sampford Courtenay were rounded up and the most important of them sent up to London for trial. Others were executed at Exeter, although the Government advised Russell to spare 'the common and mean men'. Among those who died was Robert Welsh, Vicar of Cowick, one of the best strongbowmen in the rebel ranks, who, as is well-known, was hanged in chains on the top of his own church tower, in his vestments, with a holy water bucket, a sprinkler, a sanctus bell and a rosary tied to him. Two priests whose office in the rebel army had been 'Governor of the Camps' also suffered at the hands of the executioner. These and three other executed priests whose names we know were probably not parochial incumbents. Only two such are mentioned in the registers of the Diocese of Exeter, which included Devon and Cornwall, as having been attainted. There is good evidence to suppose that two others were executed, but it seems that altogether very few of the incumbents of the 520 or so parishes in the diocese took an active part in the battle to preserve the Mass they had said week in, week out for years – a struggle in which some 4,000 of their fellow West-countrymen are said to have perished.

The Western Rebellion was not the only revolt in the year 1549. One in Yorkshire has already been referred to. Another in Buckinghamshire and Oxfordshire started because the local clergy were annoyed by the views being propounded by Peter Martyr in the university city. Here too church towers were ornamented with priests' corpses.

Far more important was the uprising which took place in Norfolk – Kett's Rebellion. Just as in the West Country what was primarily a religious rising produced economic demands, so here what was primarily caused by economic troubles had religious overtones, though in this case they were radical, not reactionary, in character. It was the fashion to blame all social and economic distress on the enclosure of arable and common land for sheeprearing, and this fashion spread as a result of the lecturing and pamphleteering of a group of reforming clerics and do-gooders who were known as the Commonwealth Party. Among them were Bishop Hugh Latimer, Thomas Lever and Robert Crowley. They got the Protector on their side, and he condemned enclosure by proclamation and sent commissioners out to investigate the situation and enforce existing laws against the practice, which local magistrates who were enclosers themselves, were loath to implement. Apparently, by doing this, Somerset created the impression that he would assist the oppres-

sed against their landlords, and Kett's Rebellion was an attempt
to get his support against the Norfolk gentry. Robert Kett,
tanner and landowner, had 16,000 men on Mousehold Heath,
outside Norwich, where Matthew Parker, a future Primate of
All England, preached to them under the 'Oak of Reformation'
and a local priest said the daily office from the new Prayer Book.
They did not intend to move on to the capital like the Devonshire rebels but to deprive the local magistrates of their powers
and, in the name of the King, establish their own communist
state in rural East Anglia.

Like the Western rebels, those of East Anglia produced their
manifesto for the Government's attention. They condemned
enclosures, rack-renting and the general failure of the Norfolk
magistracy to enforce the 'good laws, statutes and proclamations'
of the Tudor governments. They wanted their common rights
protected, and free fishing in the rivers. There was much else of
an economic nature in the rebels' demands, but it is more appropriate to our purpose for us to examine the religious complaints
and notice the effect that continental Protestantism was having
in the east of the country, where it had taken root in soil
prepared by the Lollards. Most striking is an article in which it
is requested that all bondmen may be free, for God made all free
with His precious blood-shedding. It was an appeal which had
also featured in the Twelve Articles issued during the great
Peasants' Revolt against serfdom in Germany in 1525. There
was a demand for the ejection of priests unable to preach, and a
suggestion that they might be replaced by clergy elected by the
individual congregations which also bore a striking resemblance
to an article of the German peasants. Other articles contained
old grievances about pluralism and tithes, which the rebels
wanted commuted to a money payment of 3p in the noble (33p).
They wanted all incumbents to reside and none to be gentlemen's chaplains. They thought that all clergy with benefices
worth £10 a year or more should justify their claim to a good
stipend by teaching poor children the Catechism and Prymer.
They seem to have disliked the idea of any cleric owning property.
They demanded that no priest should buy any more and that

the lands in the clergy's possession should be let to laymen. However, they did not want laymen to be able to take any benefices to farm. One of the chief purposes of these articles was probably to ensure residence.

Somerset adopted similar tactics with the Norfolk rebels to those taken with the South-Westerners. First, the local gentry were sent to persuade them to disperse, one of them taking three cartloads of beer with him to help win their confidence. Then a government herald offered them a general pardon if they would go home. The night he arrived the rebels began a bombardment of Norwich. Three days later the city was in their hands. The next to try his luck with a pardon was the Lord Lieutenant of Norfolk, the Marquis of Northampton, with, it is said (probably with some exaggeration), about 14,000 men to back him up. The rebels were the more persuasive, and, after they had attacked, the Marquis fled the city. The Government now decided on more determined action. All the counties around Norfolk were ordered to levy troops to fight the rebels. The Earl of Warwick took charge of them, and was soon reinforced by German mercenaries. The undisciplined rebels were no match for this army and some 3,000 are said to have died in battle. At least forty-nine others, including Kett, were executed.

[10] THE PROTESTANT HIGHTIDE

Northumberland

The rebellions of 1549 served to draw attention to the weaknesses in Somerset's system of government and to suggest that the logical conclusion of his policy was anarchy. His enemies in the Council prepared to unseat him. They had the support of the most powerful sections of the community – the landlords, who saw him as the promoter of a working-class revolt against them, and the commercial middle class, who resented his denunciation of their profits and the heavy taxes he attempted to impose on them. His attempts at reform had offended the conservative in religion, but had not earned him the support of the Reformers who were dissatisfied with the rate and extent of the progress made. Members of all sections of the community accused him of the deliberate murder of his own brother, Thomas, who had been executed on a legitimate charge of treason, and there was concern about a French threat to capture Boulogne, one of England's two small possessions on the European mainland.

The Protector was in a weak position. To the poor he was still the 'Good Duke', but their support was useless in the face of enemies who controlled a military body experienced in dealing with peasant revolt. Russell, the commander in the West, refused to obey a summons to his aid, while the army which had dealt with Kett and his followers was in the hands of his chief rival for power, John Dudley, Earl of Warwick.

On 14 October 1549, the Lord Protector was committed to the Tower. He was released early in the New Year, when Warwick, having got rid of his enemies in high places, became Lord President of the Council. With a generosity which is difficult to explain, but which could have been prompted either by memories of over twenty years of friendship and comradeship in arms or a need for the benefit of Somerset's experience in affairs of State, the victor gave the vanquished the position of Earl Marshal, and seems to have sought his cooperation in the work of government. But Somerset's reappearance heralded a new wave of popular support for him, and it grew so rapidly that is seemed likely that when Parliament met in January 1552 it would support his resumption of the supreme control of the realm. Warwick took steps to prevent this. By playing on the young King's vanity, he gained his confidence and let him attend Council meetings, where he used him against his uncle. The Lord President was created Duke of Northumberland, and Somerset was tried on a trumped-up charge of treason. There was some evidence that he had been trying to recover his position of power, but treason was not proved, and by a perversion of justice he was executed for felony the day before Parliament assembled. The

memory of what he had done to his old friend is said to have
haunted Northumberland to the grave.

Few people have a good word to say for Northumberland. His
critics point to the reversal of Somerset's policy of toleration and
a revival of harshness towards all those who sought to disrupt
the unity of the State through religious or political activities,
and to the continuance of the established policy of spoiling the
Church. Some seem to forget that toleration in Somerset's time
was sometimes more apparent than real, and that there was a
genuine fear of national disunity and civil strife. To Dr Parker,
Northumberland is 'a man singularly devoid of sincere principles
of any kind', while Professor Dickens regards him as 'one of the
least scrupulous politicians ever to rule England'. Professor
Elton does at least give him credit for trying to do something to
tackle the evils of a debased coinage, though some economic
historians would say that he was less than successful in this
respect. An American, Professor Barrett L. Beer, takes a more
favourable view of the Duke than most commentators, portray-
ing him as a conscientious ruler, depressed by the burdens of
State.

Northumberland's character is worthy of close investigation,
and his religious views particularly merit attention. His rise to
power was promoted by several conservative politicians, Thomas
Wriothesley, Earl of Southampton, the Earl of Arundel and Sir
Richard Southwell, who believed that he would reverse the progress made by Protestantism. In the event, once he had seized
power, he had Southampton dismissed from the Council, Arundel
placed under house-arrest, and Southwell imprisoned in the
Fleet, and he threw in his lot with the reforming party. John
Hooper, who was soon to become Bishop of Gloucester, hailed
him as a 'faithful and intrepid soldier of Christ' and 'a most holy
and fearless instrument of the word of God'. John Knox was less
enthusiastic and cast doubt on his sincerity. In reply, Northumberland said that he had

for twenty years stood to one kind of religion, in the same which I
do now profess; and have, I thank the Lord, past no small dangers
for it.

Others besides Knox saw reason to wonder what that 'one kind of religion' was, or if indeed he had any sort of religion at all. As we shall see, in the hour of death he was to recant his Protestantism, and blame it on 'false and seditious' preachers. Did he use religion only for selfish ends? Did he support the Protestant cause because he felt that doing so would not only gain him the confidence of his Protestant king but also bring him material success, the exaltation of his secular power above the ecclesiastical, and greater chances of plunder, or because he was convinced of the righteousness of the cause? Did he renounce it to save his life or because he was convinced he had been in error and that by recanting he would at least save his soul? These are questions which have not been satisfactorily answered.

Deprivations and replacements

As soon as Northumberland took the reins of government, steps were taken to scotch the rumour that a reaction was about to set in. An Order in Council announced:

We are informed that divers unquiet and evilly disposed persons since the apprehension of the duke of Somerset, have noised and bruited abroad, that they should have again their old Latin service, their conjured bread and water, with suchlike vain and superstitious ceremonies, as though the setting forth of the said book [of Common Prayer] had been the only act of the said duke; we therefore by the advice of the body and estate of our privy council . . . to put away all such vain expectation of having the public service, the administration of the sacraments, and other rites and ceremonies again in the Latin tongue . . . have thought good to command and charge you [the diocesan bishop] that immediately on receipt hereof, you do command the dean and prebendaries of the cathedral church, the parson, vicar, or curate and churchwardens of every parish, within your diocese, to bring and deliver unto you or your deputy . . . all antiphoners, missals . . . and ordinals after the use of Sarum, Lincoln, York, or any other private use, and that you . . . so deface and abolish that they never after may serve either to any such use, as they were provided for, or be at any time a let to the godly and uniform order, which by a common consent is now set forth.

This injunction was embodied in an Act of Parliament, which said that apart from the *Book of Common Prayer*, the only prayer book which could be used was King Henry's Prymer, and that only if the prayers to the saints had been erased from it. The result was the destruction of many priceless examples of medieval art. At the same time an assault was ordered on those statues and pictures which had somehow escaped previous orgies of destruction.

To promote the progress of Protestantism, several changes were made in the episcopal bench. Bishop Bonner was deprived of his see of London and committed to the Tower because he had not asserted from the pulpit, as he had been required to do, that the fact that the King was not of age did not interfere with his sovereign authority. He was replaced by Nicholas Ridley, who was translated from Rochester, and the diocese of Westminster was united with that of London. Gardiner, although he had shown his willingness to use the 1549 Book, was prosecuted under the Act of Uniformity, and John Ponet, who had succeeded Ridley at Rochester, was given his see. He did not, however, enjoy the revenue from its vast estates. Instead he was given a stipend of 2,000 marks a year. Bishop Tunstall, falsely charged with encouraging a conspiracy in the north, was placed under house-arrest in 1550, and in 1553 his rich diocese of Durham was divided by Act of Parliament into two parts to be governed like Winchester by salaried bishops. The estates, it is said, were intended to become a County Palatine for the Lord President. Day of Chichester, a firm believer in transubstantiation, was replaced by John Scory, an ex-Dominican who had become Cranmer's chaplain. The octogenarian Bishop of Exeter, John Veysey, was required to resign his see on account of 'his extreme old age and other considerations which he has declared to the Earl of Bedford' (Russell's new title). The King did, however, allow him to keep certain profits of the see because of 'his services to his father for twenty years or more'. The man who succeeded to the much depleted revenues of the diocese was Miles Coverdale, translator of the Bible and Russell's chaplain on his expedition against the Western rebels – a man likely to meet with a mixed reception in the unhappy south-west. Indeed there were at least two attempts

to poison him. He was, however, a most diligent pastor, speaking
from the pulpit of his cathedral on every Holy Day and reading
from the Scriptures and other theological works twice a week in
some church or other in the capital of his diocese. He also
instituted and ordained men himself, instead of leaving these
jobs to deputies. Other of the new bishops were equally diligent.
Notably so was John Hooper, Bishop of Gloucester.

Hooper had begun his career as a Cistercian monk, but had
been converted to radical views and had fled to Strasbourg to
avoid persecution under the Six Articles. He was much influenced
by Zwinglian teaching and went to live at Zurich with Zwingli's
successor Bullinger. He returned home in 1549 to become
Somerset's chaplain. When he was offered the see of Gloucester,
he at first refused to accept it. Being a fundamentalist, that is a
believer in the absolute truth of the divinely inspired Scriptures,
Hooper believed that biblical authority should be taken as final
on all issues. He could accept no ceremony as lawful which had
not been enjoined by Scripture, and moreover objected to the
service for the consecration of bishops on two specific grounds.
One was having to swear the Oath of Supremacy by God, the
Saints and the Holy Evangelists, and the other was having to
wear vestments which had acquired a significance as the emblems
of sacrifice. It was only after the saints had been removed from
the oath and Hooper had spent a spell in prison for his stubborn-
ness that this most radical of bishops was consecrated. But then
he set to work with great zeal in his diocese, making frequent
visitations and presiding in person over his diocesan court.
Like a true father-in-God he cared for the poor and tried hard
to fight the evils which resulted from non-residence – the neglect
of churches and congregations. He saw his diocese as a mission
field but lamented the lack of suitable missionaries. To Somerset's
secretary, William Cecil, he wrote,

You and I, if we should kneel all the days of our life, could not con-
dign thanks to God for that he hath mercifully inclined the hearts of
the people to wish and hunger for the word of God as they do. Doubtless it is a great flock that Christ will save in England . . . there
lacketh nothing among the people but sober, learned and wise men.

He conducted a survey of his diocese which showed him that many of his parish clergy were far from wise. Examining 311 of them on the Commandments, the Articles of the Faith and the Lord's Prayer, he found that 168 were unable to repeat the Commandments accurately, 10 were unable to repeat the Creed and 216 were unable to prove its articles by reference to Scripture. Ten could not repeat the Lord's Prayer, 39 did not know where it was to be found in the Bible and 34 did not know its author. It is perhaps indicative of how far the clergy had come to rely on direction from the Crown that one incumbent said that he knew it to be the Lord's Prayer because it had been given 'a Domino Rege' and written in the King's book of Communion Prayers. It was a sad situation which Hooper's survey revealed – an indication of how much still had to be done to reform the Church of England.

Soon after the visitation which produced these findings had taken place, Hooper's problems were increased, as his see was amalgamated with that of Worcester, and he, too, became a stipendiary. The occasion was the deprivation of Bishop Nicholas Heath for his refusal to subscribe to a new Ordinal. This book, published in March 1550, contained a service of ordination modelled on that in the Sarum Pontifical, and Bucer as well as Cranmer had a hand in its compilation. There was no mention in it of ordination to minor orders. The ministers of the reformed Church were to be bishops, priests and deacons only. And the new nature of the priesthood was clearly indicated. Those newly ordained to the priestly order were not only to be handed a chalice and paten as in times past, but also a Bible to signify that it was their duty to preach the Word of God. Previously deacons had received a book of the Gospels, but that had been to indicate their duty to read at Mass, not any preaching function. Now they were to receive a complete New Testament. More significant than the instruments delivered to the priest was the alteration in the wording of the bishop's charge. Previously it had been

Receive authority to offer sacrifice and celebrate Mass both for the living and the dead.

Now it was:

Take thou authority to preach the word of God and to minister the holy sacraments in the congregation.

The second Prayer Book

Despite the radical changes made in both the Mass and the ordination service, some of those who had accepted hospitality in England found cause to criticize their hosts for their timidity in reform. The Prayer Book Canon still included a prayer for the dead and a commemoration of the saints which were anathema to many of the Reformers. Dryander was most critical of the ambiguity of the references in the Book to the sacred elements, which he put down to the inability of the bench of bishops to agree on the matter of transubstantiation. And Bucer wrote a critical review of the Book in twenty-eight chapters.

The more radical of the native-born clergy were equally disappointed. Hooper wrote to his old friend Bullinger,

I can scarcely express to you, my dear friend, under what difficulties and dangers we are labouring and struggling that the idol of the Mass may be thrown out. It is no small hindrance to our exertions that the form which our Senate or Parliament, as we commonly call it, has prescribed for the whole realm is so very defective and of doubtful construction; and in some respects manifestly impious. I am so much offended with that book and that not without abundant reason, that, if it be not corrected, I neither can nor will communicate with the Church in the administration of the Lord's Supper.

Hooper wrote those words before he became a bishop. By the time he took his seat on the episcopal bench, several of those who had upheld transubstantiation had left it, and a 'purified' version of the Prayer Book had been prepared.

The movement towards further liturgical reform had received a stimulus from Nicholas Ridley, the new Bishop of London. He was worried about the number of priests in his diocese who were interpreting the Mass in the old way, and carrying out ceremonies in the performance of the new service which had been required by the rubrics of the old. He issued injunctions which ordered

that no minister do counterfeit the popish mass in kissing the Lord's board; washing his hands or fingers after the Gospel or the receipt of the holy communion; shifting the book from one place to another; laying down and licking the chalice after the communion; blessing his eyes with the sudary thereof, or patten, or crossing his head with the same; holding his forefingers and thumbs joined together toward the temples of his head, after the receiving of the sacrament; breathing on the bread or chalice; saying the Agnus before the communion; shewing the sacrament openly before the distribution, or making any elevation thereof; ringing of the sacring bell, or setting any light upon the Lord's board. And finally, that the minister in time of the holy communion, do use only the ceremonies and gestures appointed by the Book of Common Prayer, and none other, so that there do not appear in them any counterfeiting of the popish mass.

Ridley also exhorted his clergy to remove from their churches that symbol of sacrifice, the stone altar, and replace it with 'an honest table decently covered'. He explained why he wanted this change thus:

Now when we come unto the Lord's board, what do we come for? To sacrifice Christ again, and to crucify him again, or to feed upon him that was once only crucified and offered up for us? If we come to feed upon him, spiritually to eat his body, and spiritually to drink his blood (which is the true use of the Lord's Supper), then no man can deny but the form of a table is more meet for the Lord's board than the form of an altar.

The substitution of tables for altars took place in London in June 1550. In November the Council ordered all other dioceses to follow suit. Hooper, however, wanted to go further and seal off the chancel and put the altar in the body of the congregation so that the Lord's Supper would indeed be a memorial feast.

Despite the efforts by Council and reforming bishops to eliminate 'superstitious' practices and to emphasize the fact that the chief service of the Church was now primarily one of communion and not a sacrifice, clergy apparently continued with the old ceremonies. In 1552 an Act of Uniformity was passed which contained a tribute to the 1549 Prayer Book as

a very godly order, agreeable to the word of God and the primitive church, very comfortable to all good people desirous to live in Christian conversation, and most profitable to the state of this realm.

However, it was lamented that the people had not been attending church to hear it read and that there had

arisen in the use and exercise of the foresaid common service ... divers doubts of the fashion and ministration of the same, rather by the curiosity of the minister, and mistakers, than of any other worthy cause: therefore for the more plain and manifest explanation hereof, as for the more perfection of the said order of common service, to make the same prayer and fashion of service more earnest and fit to stir Christian people to the true honouring of Almighty God, the King's most excellent Majesty ... hath caused the foresaid order of common service, entitled The Book of Common Prayer, to be faithfully and godly perused, explained, and made fully perfect.

Professor Dickens tells us that the second and 'fully perfect' Prayer Book answered many of the objections which Bucer had made to the first, but that it did not approach the radical standpoint of à Lasco and Poullain, who had devised services for use by their congregations which were revolutionary in their departure from the original shape of the Mass. He claims that Cranmer and those who worked with him on the new book were not aiming to produce anything of a Zwinglian or Calvinist nature: Dr Parker, however, says that the fact that some of Bucer's more conservative suggestions for the retention of certain features of the 1549 Book were not accepted shows how firmly radical influences were in control, and he asserts that the changes made in the Holy Communion and other services approximated the English service, both in language and ceremonial, much more closely to continental rites of the Swiss type.

It is certain that both Archbishop and Council had been under considerable pressure from the radicals to make changes in the Prayer Book, and some of the changes made do bear some relationship to the work of à Lasco and Poullain. For example several additions based on elements in à Lasco's liturgy – an exhortation, confession and absolution – were made to the service of Matins, or Morning Prayer, as it was now called. Otherwise, apart from the introduction of alternative chants, Matins and Evensong remained unchanged. But the office of Extreme Unction and Mass for the dead were omitted altogether. The very word 'Mass' found no place in the new Book. Neither did the word 'altar', although 'priest' was retained as a description of the minister officiating at the 'Holy Table'. This was to be placed lengthways along the chancel, and the priest was not to face east, with his back to the people, like one offering a sacrifice to God, but to stand on its north side. The vestments Hooper so much objected to were abolished, and the minister was to be attired simply in a surplice. Ordinary bread was to be used instead of the round wafers, or 'hosts' of old, and what was left over was to be given to the curate for his own use.

As to the actual order of service, the introit psalm, retained by the Lutherans but abandoned by the Zwinglians and Calvinists, was left out. Emphasis was laid on the Scriptures with the introduction into the service of the Ten Commandments and responses, to signify the state of life required of the communicant. The Commandments already featured in the service used by Poullain, and it was from this source that the final response, 'And write all these Thy laws in our hearts, we beseech Thee', came. An attempt was made to eliminate everything unwarranted by Scripture – the prayer for the descent of the Holy Spirit, the commemoration of the Virgin and the saints, the prayer for the dead, the mixing of water with the wine (symbolic of the water and blood which flowed from the side of Christ on Calvary), even the sign of the Cross. The *Agnus Dei*, the hymn to the sacrificed Lamb of God which followed the consecration, was omitted, so there was no gap between the blessing of the elements and their reception by the congregation. Very significantly the words of administration spoken by the priest to the communicant:

The Body of our Lord Jesus Christ, which was given for thee, preserve thy body and soul unto everlasting life and

The Blood of our Lord Jesus Christ, which was shed for thee, preserve thy body and soul unto everlasting life

were replaced by

Take and eat this in remembrance that Christ died for thee, and feed on him in thy heart by faith with thanksgiving

and

Drink this in remembrance that Christ's blood was shed for thee and be thankful.

The new words of administration were similar to those in à Lasco's service, and the emphasis was apparently on the idea that the Communion Service was a commemorative feast. This, in the eyes of some, would seem to support Professor Powicke's view that one of the aims behind the new rite was to interpret the Sacrament of the Altar more clearly in a Zwinglian sense. Others, however, would point to the phrase 'and feed on him . . .', which does not appear in à Lasco's order, as evidence that Cranmer had been influenced by the writings, popular in the days of Reformation, of the ninth-century Benedictine, Ratramnus of Corbie, who said that

under the veil of corporeal bread and corporeal wine the spiritual body and spiritual blood exist.

Professor Dugmore discounts Zwinglian influence in the words of administration, seeing them as representative of a view of the service already taught in devotional books produced in the fourteenth and fifteenth centuries, and traces the idea of eating 'in the heart' back to Augustine. However, Dr Peter Brooks, while feeling that it is wrong to describe any reformer's position as Zwinglian at so late a stage in the development of Protestant theology, claims that Cranmer had arrived at a belief in what he calls the 'True' or Spiritual Presence as a result of considerable continental influence, and that it was in essence akin to the position held by Calvin.

Despite the changes, some of the radicals were not happy with the new rite. It was due to come into use on 1 November 1552, but in September, a Scottish chaplain, thought to have been John Knox, preached a sermon before the King in which he protested against a rubric which directed that communicants should receive the elements kneeling. As a result, the Council inserted into the Book of Common Prayer the so-called 'Black Rubric', which, while it enjoins the kneeling posture for the sake of reverence and uniformity and as a sign of grateful acknowledgment, denies any intention to adore the elements, any concession to the belief that the bread and wine did not 'remain still in their very natural substance'.

Incorporated in this second Prayer Book was a new Ordinal. It is significant that bishops were no longer to be handed a pastoral staff at their consecration, and newly ordained priests were no longer to be given a chalice. The Scriptures were the basis of the Reformed Church, and the Bible was the only instrument to be delivered to bishops and priests alike.

When the new Book was introduced non-attendance at church was for the first time made a statutory offence. Ecclesiastical punishments, including excommunication, were to be meted out to those laymen who failed to attend common prayer on Sundays and festivals. Those attending any other form of worship were to suffer six months' imprisonment for the first offence, a year for the second, and life imprisonment for the third. Attendance at church and the use of the new service were essential if the work of reformation were really to get under way amongst the people. So far the most noticeable results of the Government's reforms had been irreligion, irreverence and the looting of the Church's wealth. Indeed, in 1552 a very severe Act was passed prohibiting quarrelling and brawling in churches and churchyards; the use of a weapon in a consecrated place was to lead to the penalty of the loss of an ear. Curiously, in view of the new insistence on attendance at church, another Act of the same year, which listed all the feast days in future to be observed – with all Sundays among them – stated that it should

be lawful for any husbandman, labourer, fisherman, &c., to labour, ride, fish, or work on the foresaid holidays, not only in the time of harvest, but at any other time of the year when need shall require.

The Calvinistic Sabbath was certainly not to be part of the English scene – yet.

Whether the new Prayer Book was much used is a matter of debate. Its publication was delayed so that the Black Rubric could be inserted, and, before many parishes could have had time to acquire a copy of it, the regime which had introduced it had been overthrown. However, the Government did have time to attempt a confiscation of all those vestments and other ornaments of the Church which the simplified ritual rendered superfluous. The commissioners appointed to the task found that what they sought had in many places already disappeared. Thuribles, incense boats, altar frontals, crosses and candlesticks had all been sold and, as had happened at Exeter during the siege, the money raised had been used for the benefit of the local community. It had been spent on such worthy causes as building a market hall, digging a new harbour, repairing existing harbour walls and making a river navigable. In some places the money raised from the sale of plate had at least been put to religious purposes. At one church it had provided a new font, lectern and pulpit; at another, four pews; and at another, two buttresses to support the church wall. It had been found necessary to sell plate as the only means of getting what was needed to provide the books required for the new services, and to put scriptural texts on a wall in place of the washed-out picture of the saints. At one time parishioners would have gladly given whatever they could afford for the ornamentation of their parish church. Now many of them either disapproved the form of religion practised there or doubted whether what they gave would long avoid the clutches of a rapacious Government. In one parish at least, even though the churchwardens went so far as to sell the contents of their church house 'with the consent of the whole parish', they did have enough hope of better days to put their vestments into safekeeping instead of selling them to be cut up into bed canopies.

Churchwardens were expected to recover all goods stolen, lost or sold, or else give the Government their monetary value. Where plate had been appropriated for public works, where

they found it difficult to recover, and in cases of hardship, the
commissioners referred the matter of compensation to the Council. All confiscated plate was sent to the Jewel House in the
Tower of London, all vestments and inferior metal work were
sold locally, and, according to instructions, all linen goods were
distributed among the poor of the parishes to which they had
belonged.

The Forty-two Articles

The Church of England had been stripped of all that the Reformers regarded as superstitious; the nature of its chief service had
been changed from the sacrifice of the Body and Blood of its
Saviour, shrouded in mystery, to a memorial of the Last Supper
in which the people shared; the preaching of the Word had become
the chief duty of its ministers. It only remained now to give it a
code of law to replace the universal one of the medieval Church,
and a statement of its Faith.

As long ago as 1532, the Submission of the Clergy had provided for the setting-up of a committee to revise the Canon Law,
but nothing had come of this proposal. A commission had been
appointed for the same purpose in 1549 but its life had been
fixed for a period which had now expired. Now, a commission
of thirty-two, half clergy, half laymen, was appointed to produce a new legal code. The result of its work was the *Reformatio
Legum Ecclesiasticarum*, which reasserted the Church's right to
independent jurisdiction over both clergy and laity. There were
many who would have liked to have seen church courts abolished,
especially the common lawyers who coveted the fees their
officials received, and Northumberland himself was opposed to
the existence of a rival discipline to the law of the State. Perhaps
such opposition made it inevitable that nothing would come of
the proposals made in the *Reformatio*, but it was a change of
Government and consequent change in the official religious attitude which really sealed its fate. Some of the proposals were well
in advance of their time. They included the recognition of
adultery, desertion and ill-treatment as grounds for the divorce

of either marriage partner, and the holding of annual diocesan
conferences to be attended by laymen as well as clergy.

In 1553 the Forty-two Articles of Religion were published.
Cranmer's was the working spirit behind them. He had had past
experience of the formulation of sets of beliefs of this sort. Doubtless he still remembered the negotiations with the Lutherans in
1538, when he had been much influenced by the Confession of
Augsburg. Professor Dickens claims that he still had the thirteen
articles drawn up at that time in mind, and some of the new
Articles were indeed borrowed from the Lutheran Confession.
But the Edwardian Articles were not an attempt at a compromise
between Lutheranism and traditional Catholic doctrine, nor do
they seem to have been what Professor Elton, with obvious
uncertainty, defines them as – 'a compromise between the
Lutheran and Calvinist (or Zwinglian?) creeds'. Rather were they
a reflection of the confused state of affairs which was the product
of twenty years of Reformation, and more particularly of six
years of progressive radicalism.

Some of the Articles attacked the ways of the past – the Papal
Supremacy, purgatory, image and relic worship, prayer to the
saints, the sacrifice of the Mass. In their dislike of the notion of
salvation through good works, the compilers went so far as to
say that good works not inspired by Christ were not pleasing
to God and had 'the nature of sin'. What is more, the Calvinistic
doctrine of Predestination was affirmed with the words,

Predestination to life is the everlasting purpose of God, whereby
(before the foundations of the world were laid) he hath constantly
decreed by his judgment secret to us, to deliver from curse and damnation those whom he hath chosen out of mankind, and to bring them
to everlasting salvation by Christ, as vessels made to honour.

This seemed to imply that some men were predestined to damnation, yet such was the mixed-up state of things that elsewhere
in the Articles it was implied that Christ had died for all men,
not just for God's elect, and the Lutheran doctrine of Justification by Faith was asserted.

The way in which the Articles dealt with that other highly

controversial matter, the nature of the Sacrament, has itself caused controversy among modern-day scholars. What the relevant article said was this:

For as much as the truth of man's nature requireth that the body of one and the self same man cannot be at one time in divers places, but must needs be in some one certain place, therefore the body of Christ cannot be present at one time in many and divers places. And because (as holy Scripture doth teach) Christ was taken up into heaven, and there shall continue unto the end of the world, a faithful man ought not either to believe or openly to confess the real and bodily presence (as they term it) of Christ's flesh and blood in the Sacrament of the Lord's supper.

Dom Gregory Dix calls this article (number xxiv) 'the perfect summary of the Zwinglian belief in the Real Absence'. In it, according to Dr Parker, Cranmer 'denied categorically even the abstract possibility of any Real Presence of Christ on earth before the Last Judgment'. Such a statement, he says, could only lead to a permanent breach between right- and left-wing Protestants, and was no hopeful sign for the cause of Protestant unity which the Archbishop had so much at heart. Professor Dickens agrees that the argument used in the article was a Zwinglian one, but says that it was also used by the Lollards and that it cannot be taken to prove that Cranmer had whole-heartedly embraced Zwinglianism. He says that the whole article, of which the passage quoted above is but a part, savours more of a compromise between Cranmer and the more radical members of the formulating committee than of a real consensus of minds, and suggests that pressure was put on the Archbishop to get him to agree to it. Professor Dugmore, however, points out that, although the article denied the 'real and bodily' presence in the Sacrament of Christ's natural body and blood, it did not deny any presence whatsoever, and he believes the statements contained in the article to be perfectly in keeping with what he considers to have been Cranmer's interpretation of the Sacrament, i.e. that Christ was present in spiritual form.

No less than eighteen of the articles were neither an attempt at compromise between Faiths nor an attack on Catholic tradition, but an attack on those supposed enemies of the State and internal peace, the Anabaptists. Swiss in origin, the Anabaptist movement had been introduced into England by Netherlandish and German immigrants who had converted a number of natives of the South-eastern counties to a faith whose most universally held tenet was that baptism should only be administered to believers. Like the Lollards, however, they had no one consistent set of beliefs, and Anabaptist heresy was a label attached by the English authorities to a multitude of very radical religious ideas, all of which seemed to tend to disunity in Church and State. While the reign of Edward VI was, by the standards of the day, remarkably free from religious persecution, two people did die at the stake for so-called Anabaptist beliefs. They were Joan Bocher, alias Joan of Kent, who was a friend of Anne Askew and whose offence was denial of Christ's incarnation of the Virgin Mary, and a Dutch surgeon, George van Parris, who denied Jesus's divinity.

When the Forty-two Articles were published, appended to them was a *Short Catechism* compiled by Bishop Ponet of Winchester and designed to be taught by schoolmasters to their scholars. Despite its title it was extremely verbose and tedious, and it emphasized the predestinarian doctrine of the Articles and gave the same sort of commentary on the nature of the Sacrament. Another product of the year 1553 was a new Prymer to replace the *King's Prymer* of 1545, which had itself been reprinted with some alterations of a more Protestant nature in 1551. The publication of the new book affords further evidence of the triumph the more radical reformers had managed to achieve over the moderates. Their triumph was, however, to be short-lived.

The death of the King

The success of the Reformation depended on the life of the sickly King Edward VI – himself a most ardent Protestant. His next heir was Mary, the daughter of Henry VIII and Catherine of Aragon. Conservative, indeed papalist in religion, she had managed to have Mass said in her house despite the Act of Uniformity, and it was evident that should she succeed to the throne it would be said in every church in the land. In 1552, the King, already consumptive, suffered badly from measles and smallpox; in the spring of 1553 his weakened constitution was attacked by a cold which made his death seem imminent. Most historians of the period believe that in desperation Northumberland persuaded Edward to save England from Popery by setting aside his father's will and declaring both his sisters bastards, but Professor Jordan argues that the King himself planned the change, and that the Duke agreed to it merely out of loyalty to his Sovereign. The facts remain, however, that in Edward's will the crown was left to the descendants of his paternal aunt Mary, Duchess of Suffolk, that one of these, Jane Grey, was married to Northumberland's son, Lord Guildford Dudley, little more than a month before the King's death, and that the will was altered by an unknown hand to make Jane the King's heir.

If Northumberland's was the mind behind these rather dubious events, what were his motives? Did he plan things simply in order to preserve what Professor Elton says mattered most to him – the ascendancy of Northumberland? Or did he do what he did out of a strange sense of duty? Professor Beer has suggested that at the height of his career the Duke yearned for retirement. He did indeed ask the question,

What should I wish any longer this life, that seeth such frailty in it? Surely, but for a few children which God has sent me, which also helps to pluck me on my knees, I have no great cause to tarry much longer here.

That he did what he did because duty required it rather than because of desire for personal reward is suggested by these pitiful words:

When others went to their sups and pastimes after their travail, I went to bed with a careful heart and a weary body, and yet abroad no man scarcely had any good opinion of me.

Yet when the chance came to relinquish the reins of government and enjoy the retirement he craved, he is supposed to have instigated illegal and underhand measures which would enable him to maintain his position of power. Did he think that it was only by keeping his power that he would keep his life? Or did he think that it was his duty to save England for Protestantism? If that was his motive, we still have to explain why he recanted in the end. One cannot help wondering if, had he declared for Mary and the Catholic Faith immediately on Edward's death, he would have saved his life and perhaps even managed to retain an influential role in the counsels of state.

Unfortunately for Northumberland, when Edward did die, Mary was still a free agent. She was summoned to the King's death bed but, warned to keep away, she fled to the Duke of Norfolk's estates, where she met with an enthusiastic reception which encouraged her to send an order to the Council to proclaim her Queen. Instead, the Council, which had already proclaimed Jane, raised troops which Northumberland led against the large army gathering in support of Henry Tudor's daughter in the Eastern Counties. The area where Protestantism had put down its deepest roots was Mary's base of operations. Hereditary monarchy and the stability which it seemed to afford counted for more at this moment than did differences of religion. Mary's supporters were so great in number that the Duke had to take refuge in Cambridge, where he heard that the Council had proclaimed Mary in his absence, and his daughter-in-law's nine days' reign was over. He decided to do what seemed wise and proclaimed Mary Queen himself. It did not do him the good he might have hoped for. The first victim of a reign which was to become notorious for the number of judicial murders committed in it was John Dudley, Duke of Northumberland. And on the scaffold he made a speech recanting his heresy in which, an eyewitness tells us, he 'edified the people more than if all the Catholics in the land had preached for ten years'.

Further Reading

Professor W. K. Jordan has recently written a history of Edward VI's reign in two volumes, *Edward VI, The Young King* (Allen and Unwin,

1968) dealing with Somerset's protectorship, and *Edward VI, The Threshold of Power* (Allen and Unwin, 1970), which deals with the ascendancy of Northumberland. Another account of the reign by Dr Peter Ramsey is promised for 1973, and Dr M. L. Bush is writing a life of Somerset. There is no good biography of Northumberland in print, but there is a revealing article on his career by Barrett L. Beer, entitled 'The Rise of John Dudley, Duke of Northumberland', in *History Today*, Vol. XV, No. 4 (April 1965).

For a concise account of the religious changes of the reign see Owen Chadwick, *The Reformation* (Penguin, 1964), and for the careers of the Swiss Reformers whose work influenced them, G. R. Potter's chapter ,'Zwingli and Calvin', in Joel Hurstfield (ed.), *The Reformation Crisis* (Edward Arnold, 1965). A valuable commentary on the changes can be found in Sir Maurice Powicke's brilliant essay, *The Reformation in England* (Oxford Paperbacks, 1961). There is an unusual and somewhat dubious interpretation of the alterations made in the liturgy in H. A. L. Rice, 'Thomas Cranmer, 1489–1556, Archbishop of Canterbury' in *History Today*, Vol. VI, No. 7 (July 1956), while widely differing interpretations of Cranmer's eucharistic doctrine can be found in Gregory Dix, *The Shape of the Liturgy* (Dacre Press, 1945), C. W. Dugmore, *The Mass and the English Reformers* (Macmillan, 1958), and Peter Brooks, *Thomas Cranmer's Doctrine of the Eucharist* (Macmillan, 1965). A recent book on the story of the Prayer Book is G. J. Cuming, *A History of Anglican Liturgy* (Macmillan, 1969). It is particularly valuable in that it includes an appendix where the 1548 *Order of Communion* is given in full, together with translations of a number of continental rites. *The First and Second Prayer Books of Edward VI* have been published in the 'Everyman's Library' series (Dent/Dutton, 1910) with an introduction by E. C. S. Gibson, and are of course essential reading for any student of the subject. The present *Book of Common Prayer* is the 1552 version with modifications made in 1559, 1604 and 1662.

The Prayer Book Rebellion is dealt with in that famous study in regional history, A. L. Rowse, *Tudor Cornwall* (Macmillan, 1969). Documents relating to it and to Kett's Rebellion are transcribed in the book by Anthony Fletcher referred to on page 118. For an account of the effects of greed in high places on the fortunes of one diocese see Phyllis M. Hembry, *The Bishops of Bath and Wells, 1540–1640 – Social and Economic Problems* (Athlone Press, 1967).

Principal Events

1547. Edward VI's accession. Somerset, Lord Protector. Heresy
      and treason laws repealed. Communion in both kinds. *Congé
      d'élire* abolished. Act for the dissolution of Chantries
1548. Some ancient customs considered superstitious abolished.
      Order of Communion
1549. Marriage of clergy allowed. First *Book of Common Prayer*.
      Western Rebellion. Kett's Rebellion. Somerset overthrown
1550. Reformed Ordinal issued
1552. Second *Book of Common Prayer*. Somerset executed.
      Commission for the reformation of the ecclesiastical laws
1553. Seizure of church plate. Forty-two Articles issued. 6 July,
      Edward dies. 10 July, Jane proclaimed Queen. 20 July,
      Northumberland proclaims Mary Queen. Northumberland
      executed

PART V
Mary's Counter-Reformation

[11] THE REACTIONARY PROCESS

The new Queen

At about six o'clock on the evening of 18 July 1553, first the bells of St Paul's Cathedral, then all the church bells in London rang out to herald the beginning of a new reign. Inside the Cathedral a joyful *Te Deum* was sung; outside, people built the bonfires of rejoicing and put up tables in the streets for communal feasting. Henry Tudor's daughter was Queen of England; it seemed an event worth celebrating.

The new Queen celebrated her accession by fixing up the forbidden crucifix in the chapel of her castle at Framlingham. No one was more fervent in her faith than Mary Tudor. It was a faith she had inherited from her mother – the strict orthodoxy of Spain. It has been said that Mary was more a Spaniard than a Tudor. Indeed we have it from the ambassador Venice sent to her Court that she scorned to be English and boasted of her Spanish descent.

Her feeling for the Faith of Rome and for the homeland of Catherine of Aragon are not hard to understand when one remembers the long period of exile from Court which she shared for a time with her mother, and the indignity of being labelled a bastard – events with which England's break with the Holy See seemed most closely connected. What is perhaps surprising is that despite the ill-treatment she had suffered she retained an interest in the welfare of others and a tendency to mercy which was manifest even when the security of her throne was threatened. She was a simple soul – straightforward and generous, sincere but stubborn. It was for these last two attributes that she was to be remembered.

A new Queen sat on the throne, but the same old faces could be seen round the Council board – the faces of those who had supported and deserted Northumberland. There were, it is true, some new councillors – men who had comforted Mary in her days of adversity. Alas, their presence only succeeded in making the Council into a body which was both unwieldy and lacking in harmony. Indeed it eventually split into two rival factions. One was led by Lord Paget, who had been King Henry's Secretary of State and had received his barony for supporting Northumberland in his bid for power, but who had been out of favour towards the end of Edward's reign. The other was under the direction of the lately imprisoned Bishop of Winchester, Stephen Gardiner, now restored to his see and appointed Lord Chancellor. Rather than take advice from either party, Mary confided in and trusted the ambassador of her cousin, the Emperor Charles V, who himself had advised her throughout her troubles – Simon Renard.

It was on Renard's advice that the Queen compromised her faith in the matter of the burial of her dead brother. She feared that it would be wrong to send King Edward to his grave without the benefit of the ancient rites of the Church. However, to avoid possible trouble from the Protestants, she agreed to what the ambassador suggested and let Archbishop Cranmer read the Prayer Book service at the funeral in the Abbey, while she heard Requiem Mass in the chapel of the White Tower.

Mary seems to have felt that few of her loving subjects truly adhered to the Protestant Faith, and that those who had been misled or frightened into the new ways would, through the merciful will of God, soon return to the right path. It was for this reason that at first she embarked on a policy of toleration. On 12 August 1553 the Council was instructed to publish a declaration that albeit her Grace's conscience is stayed in matters of religion, yet she meaneth graciously not to compel or constrain other men's consciences, otherwise than God shall (she trusteth) put into their hearts a persuasion of the truth that she is in, through the opening of his word unto them by godly, virtuous and learned preachers.

One such 'virtuous and learned' preacher spoke at Paul's Cross the following day. He was Gilbert Bourne, chaplain to old Bishop Bonner, and the result of his address was a riot (possibly pre-arranged) from which he barely escaped with his life. It heralded a tougher line from the Council. Every alderman in the city was ordered to give notice to all the parishes in his ward that no minister should preach, 'make any open or solemn reading of Scripture', or let anyone else preach from his pulpit, without the Queen's licence. And the Lord Mayor was to arrest the people responsible for the riot. Several noted preachers of Protestantism were among those taken into custody.

The prohibition of unlicensed preaching was repeated in a proclamation which stated what was to be the immediate policy of the Crown in matters of religion. The Queen, it said,

cannot now hide that religion, which God and the world knoweth she hath ever possessed from her infancy hitherto, which, as her majesty is minded to observe and maintain for herself by God's grace, during her time, so doth her highness much desire, and would be glad the same were of all her subjects quietly and charitably embraced.

The proclamation went on to say that she would use no compulsion in religious matters until 'such time as further order by common assent may be taken therein' – a reference to the coming session of Parliament. Then there was another of those familiar pleas for unity, an exhortation to Englishmen to abandon

those new-found devilish terms of papist or heretic, and such like, and, applying their whole care, study and travail to live in fear of God exercising their conversations in such charitable and godly doing, as their lives may indeed express that great hunger and thirst of God's word, which, by rash talk and words, many have pretended.

The constant fear of Tudor governments that the result of freedom in religious matters would be political chaos is apparent in the section of the proclamation dealing with unlicensed preaching. Such was forbidden because

it is well-known that sedition and false rumours have been nourished and maintained in this realm by the subtlety and malice of some evil disposed persons which take upon them, without sufficient authority, to preach and to interpret the word of God after their own brain.

As well as preaching, the proclamation also forbade

the printing of false-bound books, ballads, rhymes, and other lewd treatises in the English tongue, concerning doctrine in matters now in question.

The next Sunday, Gardiner's chaplain preached with the royal licence at Paul's Cross. His subject was the 'obedience of subjects and what erroneous sects are reigning in this realm by false preachers and teachers'. That Earl of Bedford who had suppressed the supporters of the Mass in Devonshire was there, along with some other members of the Council and two hundred members of the Queen's Guard. Not surprisingly, there was no trouble.

The action the Government had swiftly taken at the first sign of trouble brought a momentary calm to the capital – and a return to the old way of things. Statues of the saints began to appear in house windows; Bishop Bonner, released from Marshalsea Gaol and back on his throne at St Paul's, celebrated a Latin Mass in the Cathedral; altar-tables were placed against the east walls of churches, not only in London, but elsewhere in the kingdom, and crosses and candlesticks were brought out of hiding to decorate them.

There was a feeling abroad that everything was going to be as it had been in King Henry's time. It was even rumoured that Cranmer had agreed to say Mass before the Queen. The Archbishop was scandalized. He issued a denial of the rumour, and he and Peter Martyr threw out a challenge in which they offered to defend the Prayer Book Communion Service, and to show

that the Mass in many things has no foundation of Christ, the Apostles, or the Primitive Church, but it is manifest contrary to the same, and contains many horrid blasphemies.

The Government's response was to commit the Archbishop to prison, to await trial on a belated charge of high treason for his part in the Jane Grey affair. Whatever the charge, it was evident that the Marian era of toleration was over. It had been a particularly short one.

Deprivation and emigration

Before Cranmer's arrest the Council had already started to remove from their positions of power those bishops who seemed likely to oppose the reactionary measures the Queen desired. Its first ecclesiastical act in the new reign had indeed been to appoint a commission to deprive all bishops, deans, dignitaries and parochial ministers who had during the last two reigns succeeded to any preferment of which the old incumbent was still living. Ridley and Ponet had made way for Bonner and Gardiner; Hooper of Gloucester and Coverdale of Exeter had been summoned to the capital and lodged in the Fleet for debt to the Crown. Hooper had been given the chance to escape abroad instead of obeying his summons, though he had not taken it, and the King of Denmark had little difficulty in persuading the English Government to let Coverdale go to his country.

Some bishops who had served under Edward but had not been intruded into the place of others continued to hold office. One was Thomas Goodrich, Bishop of Ely, who was reputed to be a member of the reforming party. Hooper said that in his conversations with him he had 'discovered nothing but what was pure and holy', and counted him as one of the six bishops who were 'favourable to the cause of Christ and held right opinions on the Eucharist'. He was Lord Chancellor in Northumberland's régime and signed a letter of the Council refusing to acknowledge Mary's right to the throne. Yet, after signing a Council declaration ordering the Duke to disarm, he was pardoned by the new Queen and allowed to retain his diocese. It is noteworthy that all the bishops who did keep their sees had been consecrated to their office in King Henry's reign. No one raised to the episcopate in Edward's reign was permitted to do so.

It seems that the Council did its best to make opportunities for the radical clergy to go into exile, so that they would not be a source of embarrassment to the Crown. Even some Protestant preachers were recommending a general exodus. Despite the challenge he and Cranmer had issued, Peter Martyr asked for his passport and left. À Lasco went too, taking his congregation with him, and so did Poullain and the Glastonbury weavers. The Mayors of Dover and of Rye were ordered to let all Frenchmen leave the country freely unless individuals were excepted. Bishop Scory, the deprived Bishop of Chichester, and Bishop Bale of the Irish see of Ossory were among the native clergy who, in Cranmer's words, fled 'the infection of the anti-Christian doctrine by departure out of the realm'. In all there were some eight hundred English refugees. The laymen who went were mainly students, gentry, merchants and their families. Only about fifty working-class men are known to have gone. About seventy of the exiles were clergymen, among them some leading scholars from the universities. One was Dr Richard Cox, Dean of Christ Church, Oxford, who had been the late King's tutor and had sat on both Prayer Book commissions. From Cambridge were another of the King's tutors, John Cheke, Provost of King's, and Thomas Lever, Master of St John's, and the Vice-Chancellor, Edward Sandys.

Wherever they went, be it Frankfurt, Strasbourg, Emden, Zürich or Wesel, the refugees had their own places of worship where they used the Prayer Book of 1552. At Frankfurt, however, where the English congregation shared Valérand Poullain's French Church of the White Ladies, the Prayer Book was re-modelled on Calvinist lines, the Litany, oral responses and other features which seemed to be relics of Popery being omitted. John Knox was summoned to minister in the Frankfurt church but found himself opposed in his efforts to abolish still more sections of the Prayer Book, including the *Te Deum*, by a group led by Dr Cox. Cox gained the support of the city authorities, and Knox left for Geneva. However, Cox's party produced a *Book of Discipline* for the Frankfurt congregation which was more Swiss than English in character. Elders were to be appointed to act as censors of manners and a number of deacons were to assist the pastor in his care for the poor and the sick. After a dispute about the powers of the pastor over his congregation, a further book was formulated which made the congregation the source of all authority. Thus, some people would believe, was born English Congregationalism or Independency.

Other congregations were more orthodox. Bishop Scory ministered to that at Emden, and Jewel, who was one day to be a bishop himself, at Zürich. Another bishop, Ponet, was to preach at Strasbourg after the way had been prepared for the establishment of an English colony by Peter Martyr. There the Bishop published a *Short Treatise of Politic Power*, in which, possibly with Mary in mind, he asserted that in certain circumstances the killing of a tyrant by a sovereign people given their authority by God was justified. At Geneva both John Knox and former Cambridge professor Christopher Goodman wrote books in which they said that rebellion against idolatrous and ungodly rulers was a duty. At Geneva too, work started on a new version of the Bible – one in which the chapters were divided into numbered verses. It is commonly known as the 'Breeches Bible' because of the strange translation of *Genesis*, iii, 7, where we are told that Adam and Eve, on becoming aware of their nakedness, made themselves 'breeches'. Knox was free to produce the sort of Prayer Book he wanted. Known as the Genevan Service Book, it had the blessing of Calvin himself. Another refugee, John Foxe, went to live in Basle, where he began to record the sufferings of those of like mind who had stayed behind in England.

Parliamentary processes and royal injunctions

On 1 October Mary was crowned Queen, and in addition to taking the usual oaths she pledged herself to maintain the rights of the Holy See. Four days later, after the ancient and still illegal Mass of the Holy Ghost had been sung in St Margaret's, Westminster, she opened her first Parliament. Gardiner, as Chancellor, declared to the assembled members the Queen's intention to restore the Pope's authority. It might appear an odd thing for

the author of *De Vera Obedientia* to have done, but he had seen
what at first seemed to be merely the substitution of an English
authority over the Church for a foreign one lead to the abolition
of the Mass and his own imprisonment. Perhaps he felt that submission to Rome would be a safeguard against this happening
again.

What had been done by Parliament had to be undone by
Parliament, but the Pope's authority was not restored by that
first Marian assembly, despite the Lords' apparent willingness
to agree to this move. A return to the Roman fold seemed to the
Commons to foreshadow the loss of the lands Henry's headship
of the Church had placed in their laps. However, the sentence
of annulment pronounced by Cranmer on the marriage of the
Queen's parents was denounced as 'corrupt and unlawful',
and her legitimacy was established. And, after a week's 'marvellous dispute', all the religious legislation of her brother's reign –
the two Acts of Uniformity, and those dealing with the election
of bishops, the marriage of priests, the removal of images and the
keeping of festivals – were repealed. The reason given was the
familiar one of the need for unity in the State, for

by divers and several Acts . . . as well the divine service and good
administration of the sacraments, as divers other matters of religion,
which we and our forefathers found in this Church of England, to us
left by the authority of the Catholic Church, be partly altered and in
some part taken from us, and in place thereof new things imagined
and set forth by the said Acts, such as a few of singularity have of
themselves devised, whereof has ensued amongst us, in a very short
time, numbers of diverse and strange opinions and diversities of sects,
and thereby grown great unquietness and much discord.

It was enacted that, after 20 December next, no service should
be used in England other than those which had been in use in the
last year of the reign of Henry VIII.

The Prayer Book had been outlawed, but that does not mean
to say that it was no longer used. In the capital itself, there were
regular meetings of from forty to two hundred people at which
Holy Communion was celebrated according to the English rite.

The officiant was Edmund Scambler, who, when Mary's reign was over, was to be appointed to the see of Norwich. These illegal services were held in inns, in private houses, even on board a ship anchored in the Thames. There were other communities of Prayer Book worshippers at Colchester and in other parts of the eastern counties, in the Midlands, and even in conservative Lancashire. At least one parish priest administered the Holy Communion according to both English and Latin rites. In some places those who wanted to hear the Prayer Book service had to rely on the ministrations of a minister who had been deprived of his living.

It had been estimated that a quarter of the English clergy – some 2,000 or so – were, following an injunction of March 1554, deprived for marriage. Those priests who had been monks or friars were considered to have offended against their vows of chastity and were forced to give up their wives; in the same way former nuns were made to leave their husbands. Those who had always been secular clergy had the choice of either staying married and living the life of a layman, or putting away their wives, doing public penance and taking a new living. More bishops were deprived, among them the Archbishop of York, Robert Holgate. John Bird, last Provincial of the English Carmelites and Bishop of Chester, was another who lost his see. However, he separated from his wife, and cropped up again as Bonner's assistant bishop and Vicar of Dunmow. Paul Bush, formerly Provincial of the Bonhommes, lost his diocese of Bristol but ended his days as Rector of Winterbourne. Bishop Barlow of Bath and Wells, imprisoned like Hooper and Coverdale at the beginning of the reign for debt, actually resigned his see. He also submitted to interrogation on his religious views and, by ignoring the dictates of his conscience, passed the test. Eventually, however, he thought better of what he had done and fled the country. The men who replaced the out-going bishops included a number of notable academics, and John Holyman, the new Bishop of Bristol who, as a monk of Reading Abbey had been an outspoken critic of King Henry at the time of the 'divorce' proceedings, was a famous preacher.

In the diocese of York about a tenth of the beneficed parish clergy were married. In the county of Essex, where Protestant influences were strong, about 88 out of 319 beneficed priests were deprived. Even in the conservative diocese of Exeter, at least 41 of about 530 livings were vacant in 1554 through deprivation, 5 of those deprived gaining new livings during Mary's reign. More Exeter clergy may have been deprived, for 41 other benefices are described in the diocesan register under the year 1554 simply as *iam certo modo vacante*, where normally a full explanation of the reason for a vacancy was given. One of the positions so described is an archdeaconry which was held by a priest who is known to have been condemned for heresy.

The injunction which ordered the deprivation of married priests was one of eighteen which the bishops were required to enforce in the spring of 1554. Number XV read:

touching such persons as were heretofore promoted to orders after the new sort and fashion of order, considering they were not ordered in very deed, the bishop of the diocese finding otherwise sufficiency and ability in these men, may supply that thing which wanted in them before; and then, according to his discretion, admit them to minister.

The Exeter register affords evidence of two clerics ordained by Coverdale according to the 1552 ordinal being re-ordained with the Latin rite. But not only did one of Coverdale's ordinands remain unmolested in his living apparently without having to go through any new ceremony of ordination, another Edwardian ordinand became a prebendary of Exeter Cathedral. Perhaps some bishops only bothered to ordain ministers of the Gospel to the sacrificial priesthood when the ministers themselves asked them to.

The deprivations and the immediate lack of new ministers led to the following instruction being included in the injunctions:

Item, that every bishop ... do take order and direction with the parishioners of every benefice where priests do want, to repair to the next parish for divine service; or to appoint for a convenient time, till other better provision may be made, one curate to serve in divers

parishes, and to allot to the said curate for his labour some portion
of the benefice that he so serves.

Some bishops were probably anxious to fill their empty benefices so that their priests would not be overburdened with work,
but they were warned to

have a vigilant eye, and use special diligence and foresight, that no
person be admitted or received to any ecclesiastical function, benefice,
or office, being a sacramentary [a disbeliever in the Real Presence],
infected or defamed with any notable kind of heresy or other great
crime.

The bishops and their officers were to be on the outlook for
heresy, 'especially among the clergy' and were to correct and
punish offenders. Schoolmasters were to be examined, and removed if found suspect. In their place were to be put men who
would instruct the children in the responses to be made at
Mass.

Two other injunctions were the result of Mary's anxiety to
rid herself of the embarrassing title of Head of the Church. She
had already begun to use 'etc' after her other titles instead of it;
now she made it clear that she did not want her bishops to qualify
their official acts with the phrase, 'sanctioned by royal authority'.
Nor did she want any person entering into an ecclesiastical office
to take the oaths relating to Supremacy and succession.

It was ordered that the holy-days and fast days which had
existed at the end of King Henry's reign were to be observed,
and that the old ceremonies of baptism and confirmation should
be carried out. And the bishops were to compel their people to
attend church.

There were those who not only refused to attend church but
made trouble for those who did. There was popular agitation
for the restoration of the English Prayer Book both in Essex and
in Kent, where a priest had his nose cut off. A London merchant
attacked a preacher who had declared that the New Religion
meant the damnation of souls. Another preacher was heckled
and jostled for a sermon on the Real Presence. At a *Corpus
Christi* procession in the city a joiner attacked the priest and

tried to tear the Host from his hand. A church in Suffolk was set on fire while Mass was being sung, and this despite a punitive act passed by Parliament against those who disturbed preachers or priests celebrating Mass, or who sought to abuse the Sacrament or deface altars and church ornaments. On the day that Parliament rose, a dead dog with a shaven crown and a rope round its neck was slung through the window of the Queen's presence chamber.

While in the East of England the nation seemed divided against itself, in other more conservative parts of the country people were joyfully restoring something of the old beauty to their churches. The commissioners who had been ordered to confiscate church plate were now required to restore what they could. Those churches which could not get their old goods back bought new plate and missals, and sent their Prayer Book and *Paraphrases* away for burning. Large items of church furniture like altars and rood screens and crucifixes were not immediately restored, for they were costly and perhaps some churchwardens did not expect the new religious settlement to be permanent. In one West-country parish, however, not only did the parishioners bring their church's vestments out of hiding, but, as the Vicar gladly recorded, in the church accounts,

of divers . . . persons here was received pageants and books; and divers other things concerning our rood loft, like true and faithful Christian people, was restored to this church; by the which doings it showeth that they did like good catholic men.

He also noted that people who had loaned money to pay the church's debts reduced their demands and some even refused to be repaid. Such was the effect that the change in religion had on his parishioners that, for the first time since 1547, they presented him with gifts – a new missal, a manual (a gift of the wives of the parish), and a wafer box – and a subscription list was opened for a new paten. How happy Christopher Trichay must have been to be able to record all this. He had witnessed much sadder changes and was to see another time of heart-break before he died, after fifty-three years as Vicar of Morebath, in 1573.

The Spanish Match

Perhaps the majority of Englishmen welcomed the return of the old ways in religion which the new reign had brought. They did not, however, approve the Queen's choice of a bridegroom. Her counsellors had urged matrimony upon her. The idea of a woman ruling alone was one which took a lot of getting used to, and many felt that the Queen ought to marry in order to provide an undisputed male heir. Mary herself distrusted her own ability to rule England unaided and wanted a husband who would take some of the responsibility of government from her. More than that, perhaps, she hoped for a son who would carry on with the work she had begun. The accession of Anne Boleyn's daughter, Elizabeth, would mean the undoing of the connection with Rome she hoped to effect.

Marriage to an Englishman would mean marriage to a commoner and the jealousy of other commoners. And neither of the two native suitors who were seriously suggested – Reginald Pole, cardinal and staunch opponent of the break with Rome, and the foolish young Earl of Devon – although they were of the blood royal, were ideal consorts. Mary's Spanish heart did not need a great deal of persuading by ambassador Renard that the man for her was the Emperor Charles's son Philip, who was himself very much a Spaniard. Charles, it is said, wanted the match so that England would defend his beloved homeland, the Netherlands, against French aggression. There had for a long time been an economic tie between this country and the Netherlands, upon which the friendship between the Tudor and Hapsburg houses had been built. In 1550 the Antwerp market had collapsed and English merchants had begun to seek new outlets for their goods further afield. The tie had been loosened and Englishmen were not eager to see their country linked with any continental power, for it seemed inevitable that such a link would lead to involvement in continental politics and continental warfare. A Spanish husband for the Queen would mean a Spanish king for England, a Spanish foreign policy, the Spanish Inquisition. Gardiner, fearing a set-back to the cause of reunion with Rome, was against the marriage, so was Parliament, and so was the French ambassador, who did his best to prevent his country's old enemies from coming together in this way. Of Englishmen of influence, Paget, Gardiner's rival for dominance in the Council, was most for the match, and he worked hard to persuade his fellow councillors to give their support to the venture.

The marriage treaty was concluded in January 1554. On paper it appeared quite favourable to England. Philip was to have the title of King and a share in the government but Mary alone was to appoint to offices in Church and State, and only Englishmen were to fill them. England was not to be committed to a Hapsburg foreign policy, nor was she to be required to assist in any war in which the Imperial House was involved.

Despite the nature of its terms, the treaty brought to a head the discontent which the French ambassador and his henchmen had been carefully cultivating. Although armed risings had been planned to take place in Devon, Leicestershire, Kent and Wales, only the one in Kent came to anything. There, Sir Thomas Wyatt took charge of 3,000 men bound for the Capital. Among his officers was John Ponet, the deprived Bishop of Winchester. The Bishop's presence suggests that the rising may have been Protestant as well as anti-Spanish in character, but while Wyatt himself had Protestant sympathies and his support was drawn from an area in which the new religion was strong, his followers came from both religious parties and were united by a feeling of patriotism. Stopped at London Bridge, the rebels crossed the Thames at Kingston and got as far as Fleet Street before they surrendered to the superior royal forces. The Queen wished to show mercy to the insurgents, but, although some were pardoned, Wyatt and many others were executed at the suggestion of the Emperor Charles and the Council, as an example to other would-be rebels. Wyatt was a brave soldier, but apparently he turned coward when a judicial death threatened and betrayed others, including the Princess Elizabeth, on whose behalf he had allegedly risen, and the Earl of Devon, who, it was said, was to have been married to her. They were both sent to the Tower, but despite Renard's doubts about Philip's safety if they were allowed to live, Mary refused to let them die. Jane Grey's father had been involved in the plot, and he suffered for it, as did two of his brothers. The opportunity was also taken to get rid of Jane and her husband, who, although not themselves involved, were possible figure-heads for future uprisings.

When the danger had passed, Mary's second Parliament met and consented to the marriage. When, however, Gardiner proposed that Mary should be allowed to disinherit Elizabeth and bequeath the crown by will, the prospect of a Spanish king regnant deterred both Houses from giving their consent. Other measures introduced by the Chancellor were also defeated. They included a bill for the revival of the anti-Lollard laws and the Six Articles, which was rejected as a result of the quarrel of Paget and the lay peers with Gardiner and the bishops being transferred from Council Chamber to House of Lords. A bill for the restoration of the old bishopric of Durham was passed despite considerable opposition in the Commons. However, the attempt of the clerical party to restore the monasteries was defeated. Not only did lay lords and commons fear the loss of their ex-monastic property, they also disliked the possibility of the revival of a clerical majority in the Upper House.

Gardiner, who was convinced that peace would not come to England until order was restored to the Church, had had another bill in mind – one for the discontinuance of the title of Supreme Head of the Church. When he had raised the matter in Council, there had been an immediate outcry from those members of the Council who feared it to be what Gardiner himself intended – a prelude to the restoration of papal authority and the confiscation of their Church lands. Renard had thought that it was too dangerous a project for that particular time, and caring little what title the Queen had, providing Philip might safely come to England, he had used all his influence with Mary to have the measure dropped.

Philip came in peace in July 1554 and the royal couple were married in Winchester Cathedral on the 25th. The new King of England was a young man of 27, conscientious and slow-witted, by nature reserved and unbending, yet as capable of inspiring affection as he was of inflicting physical and mental cruelty. On the advice of his father he carefully cultivated affability and tried to make himself pleasing to the English, the nation he had come to lead into the Hapsburg alliance and back into the waiting arms of the Holy Father of Rome. With him came those who were to assist him in his sacred task – Bartholomeo de Carranza, who had represented Spain at the Council of Trent; Pedro de Soto, the Emperor's confessor; Alphonso y Castro, Philip's chaplain and an Observant Franciscan; and Juan de Villagarcia, a Dominican. It is said that Carranza, who became the Queen's confessor and Visitor of the universities of Oxford and Cambridge, tried to persuade Mary to establish the Inquisition in England. If this is true it is ironic that he was to spend the last sixteen years of his life in the dungeons of the Holy Office. Castro, however, from dubious motives, was actually to denounce vindictive proceedings against heretics from the pulpit. De Soto succeeded Peter Martyr as Regius Professor at Oxford. He had had considerable experience in dealing with heretics in Flanders and was perhaps regarded as specially suitable for similar work in England. Villagarcia, who had a high reputation as a theologian in his own country, was also given a chair at Oxford so that he could dislodge the Lutheran and Calvinist heresies from the minds of fellow dons and under-graduates.

Reginald Pole

In November 1554 another agent of the Holy See landed in England. It was Reginald Pole, whom we first met as Dean of Exeter, on his journey to France to get support from the universities for King Henry's annulment, whom we have observed waiting for his call to England from the Pilgrims of Grace and his opportunity to bring the lost sheep back to the fold, and whom we have lately seen being considered as a possible husband for the Queen of England. It is appropriate now for us to look at his interesting career more closely.

He was the grandson of George, Duke of Clarence, that brother
of Edward IV and Richard III who was drowned in the butt of
malmsey wine; and he had enjoyed the favour of King Henry
VIII, who had taken an interest in the studies which he pursued
at Oxford, Paris and Padua. Linacre was one of his teachers and
he knew several of the chief Italian scholars. Erasmus hailed
him as an 'ornament of scholarship', and one would not perhaps
be too far short of the mark if one regarded him as being of the
same school as Erasmus and those early advocates of Church
reform, Colet and More. On Wolsey's death he had the chance
of the archbishopric of York, but did not like the way the 'divorce'
proceedings were leading and returned to Italy to live a life of
learned ease. He was still only in minor orders, but such was his
obvious concern for the well-being of the Church that, in 1536,
Pope Pius III not only raised him to the diaconate, but made him
a cardinal. He was given a seat on a commission appointed to
produce a memorandum on Church reform – *Consilium de
Emendanda Ecclesia*. The commission denounced monastic
abuses, the misuse of episcopal authority, the avarice and irres-
ponsibility of the cardinals, and the claim that the Pope, even
if he sold benefices, could not commit the sin of simony. It
recommended that residence be made obligatory and that a
certain standard should be exacted of persons nominated to
benefices. His Eminence was to remember the commission's
recommendations when he returned to England. King Henry's
wrath at Pole's ultimate defection to Rome, symbolized by his
acceptance of the red hat, led to the Cardinal's attainder and the
execution of his mother, the Countess of Salisbury, and of his
eldest brother, Lord Montague. What would the King have
thought had he seen his protégé in the running for the papal
tiara, as he was in 1549? Much as he may have wanted to become
Pope, however, Pole had a more cherished ambition – to reconcile his native land to Rome.

He had been waiting across the Channel for close on a year
and a half, waiting till the Emperor and his son were sure that
his arrival would do nothing to thwart their plans. It was known
that he – although in the eyes of some Englishmen himself a

suitor for the royal hand – had advised the Queen to maintain
a holy virginity. She had not chosen to follow his advice in this
respect, but so alike were they in temperament and religious
zeal that he was to become her chief confidant and spiritual
guide in the coming months. And he was not an advocate of
caution as Charles was. He told the Queen he considered it
impudent and sacrilegious to say that matters of religion should
be carefully handled and left till the throne was safely established.

For Pole, his journey to England was an errand of mercy. The
country lay under an interdict – a papal sentence which cut the
people off from the sacraments of the Church – and those who
died unabsolved were in peril of damnation. He was coming as
Legate with papal authority to lift that interdict, but even when
Philip and Mary were safely married he was not allowed in. In
law he was a traitor, and until Parliament lifted his attainder
he could not come home. But there was more to it than that.
The nobility and gentry of England still feared that reconciliation with Rome would mean the loss of their ex-monastic lands,
for Church land was inalienable by canon law. Indeed Pole
himself desired their restoration to the Church. In the end the
Pope agreed to surrender all right to hear appeals in the matter
of such property and the Council were persuaded into letting the
Cardinal come.

Reconciliation

On 12 November 1554 Philip and Mary opened the third Parliament of the Queen's reign. Mary had done her best to secure
the return of men of the 'wise, grave, and catholic sort'. Having
been reassured on the matter of the Church lands, they reversed
Pole's attainder and passed a statute to safeguard the holders of
former ecclesiastical property against any papal afterthoughts
or subtleties of canon law. All the Cardinal could do was appeal
to conscience. However, he had something more important to
concern himself with than the restoration of the monasteries –
the restoration of the people to a state of grace. Both houses of
Parliament petitioned for reconciliation with the Holy See,

declaring themselves 'very sorry and repentant of the schism
and disobedience committed in this realm'. Then in Westminster
Hall on 30 November, after final intercession by Philip and Mary,
Lords and Commons knelt while Gardiner gave them absolution
on the Legate's authority. Six days later Convocation submitted
to the Legate, and also received absolution. On the first Sunday
in Advent, King and Queen attended a High Mass in St Paul's
Cathedral, and the Chancellor, speaking for the people of England, renounced and repented his and their past sins. Throughout
all these proceedings only one man had had the courage to object.
That was Sir Ralph Bagnall, who, when the Commons' vote
was taken on submission to the Pope, had refused his support
because he

was sworn to the contrary to King Henry VIII, which was a worthy
Prince, and laboured twenty-five years before he could abolish [the
Pope] . . . and to say I will agree to it, I will not.

Those M.P.s who did agree to it went on to repeal all the
statutes passed against papal authority since 1529, Supremacy,
Appeals, Annates, and all. In the Act which did this the story
of the schism was recited and Parliament's sorrow recorded.
Pole's act of absolution was also mentioned, and there was the
inevitable petition urging him to leave in the possession of their
new owners all the goods and rights of the Church alienated
during the schism. Convocation had already been asked and had
agreed to renounce the claims the English clergy had to them,
and the reasons for agreement given in their supplication to the
Legate, which were included in the statute too, make good
sense:

We freely confess ourselves to know well how difficult and almost
impossible would be the recovery of ecclesiastical possessions on
account of the many and almost inextricable contracts and disposal
made thereof, and that it should be attempted, the peace and tran-
quillity of the realm would be easily disturbed, and the unity of the
Catholic Church – which now by the piety and authority of your
majesties, is in your kingdom introduced – would, with the greatest
difficulty, be able to attain its due progress and end.

Also included in the statute was a dispensation from Pole which ratified, subject to the Pope's confirmation, the Henrician and Edwardian foundation of hospitals and schools, and the elevation of churches to cathedral status and the accompanying division of dioceses. The Cardinal also consented to acknowledge the right of those ordained and instituted 'by pretended authority of the Supremacy of the English Church' to keep their orders and benefices. He agreed too to ratify the sentences of the Church courts and confirm the titles of those holding alienated Church property. He ended with a plea to the new owners of ecclesiastical property to make due provision for the maintenance of the parish clergy. The Act continued with a threat of the penalties of *Praemunire* for anyone attempting to deprive the new owners of their possessions. To increase public devotion, however, such owners might during the next twenty years grant lands and titles to religious foundations without obtaining the royal licence.

Papal bulls were given legal force again, but only those

not containing matters contrary or prejudicial to the authority, dignity or pre-eminence royal or imperial of the realm, or to the laws of this realm now being in force, and not in this present Parliament repealed.

It was made clear that nothing in the Act diminished the ancient royal prerogative and that the papal authority restored in England was such as had existed at the beginning of King Henry's reign, 'without dimunition or enlargement of the same'. England's 'Parliament Pope' (as Bishop Jewel was later to call him) was to be subject to the laws passed by his creators.

Persecution

Although Mary rejoiced that her kingdom had been reunited with the Holy See, and, mistakenly, that she was soon to bear an heir who would make sure that union was maintained, she had much to worry about. Attacks on priests continued; a cat was hanged in Cheapside dressed in priestly vestments with an

imitation Host between its paws; the exiles, with whom the
London dissenters were in league, sent scurrilous literature into
the country. Bishop Bonner had issued a number of articles in
connection with a visitation of his diocese in which he dealt
with such usual matters as the good example the clergy should
set their people by avoiding ale-houses and taverns. Nine of the
articles, however, dealt with more contentious questions, such
as the marriage of priests, the use of the English service and the
refusal of the laity to attend Mass. These provoked a reply from
the exiled Bishop Bale in which he told his readers that 'This
limb of the devil and working tool of Satan, bloody Bonner,
seeketh here to deprive you of faith, true doctrine, and God's
religion'. To the Bishop and his colleagues he posed the question,

What is thy idolatrous mass and lowsy Latin service, thou sow's
belly swillbowl, but the very draught of Antichrist and dregs of the
devil?

Then he went on to tell them what he thought of them:

I think there are not greater devils than you be, neither yet more
manifest adversaries to the truth of God ... Be ashamed of thy
blasphemous doings thou most beastly bellygod, and damnable
dunghill with thy golden pillows before thee.

Other writings from abroad called for the Queen's death, and
it is said that those who held the Prayer Book services in secret
in London added a new intercession, namely that God would 'turn
the heart of Queen Mary from idolatry – or shorten her days'.

Perhaps these events and that old wish of Tudor governments
for unity in the realm had some bearing on the introduction of
that Act of Mary's third Parliament which read:

For the eschewing and avoiding of errors and heresies, which of late
have risen, grown and much increased within this realm, for that the
ordinaries have wanted authority to proceed against those that were
infected therewith: be it therefore ordained and enacted by authority
of this present Parliament, that the Statute made in the fifth year of
the reign of King Richard II, concerning the arrest and apprehension
of erroneous and heretical preachers, and one other Statute made in
the second year of the reign of King Henry IV, concerning the repress-

ing of heresies and punishment of heretics, and also one other Statute made in the second year of the reign of King Henry V concerning the suppression of heresy and Lollardy, and every article, branch and sentence contained in the same three several Acts, and every of them, shall from the twentieth day of January next coming be revived, and be in full force, strength, and effect to all intents, constructions and purposes for ever.

On 29 January 1555 the Cardinal Legate issued his commission to Bishops Gardiner, Tunstall, Capon, Thirlby and Aldridge to proceed to the trial of heretics. Before them, sitting at St Mary Overy Church, Southwark, were brought John Rogers, Prebendary of St Paul's and editor of Matthew's Bible, and John Hooper, lately Bishop of Gloucester. Both were sentenced to death, and Rogers was the first to suffer. He was burnt at Smithfield on 4 February. Hooper was sent to die in his old cathedral city. Perhaps it was believed that an example or two would be a sufficient deterrent to the Queen's opponents, but it was not. Before Mary's death brought persecution to an end, nearly 300 people were to suffer death at the stake. About a third were clergymen; 60 of them were women. Most of them were common folk from those urban and industrial centres in which Protestantism most easily took root, many of their fellows from the higher social classes having had the foresight to leave the country before persecution began. Some died for upholding what had been the official teaching of the English Church in the reign of the Queen's brother, others for professing the Anabaptism which had been anathema even then. England had never seen such persecution. The century and a quarter before 1529 had seen perhaps 100 Lollard martyrs, and during the first twenty years of Reformation some 60 persons had been executed for religious reasons, only 2 of them in King Edward's reign. Now some 70 people died each year that Mary lived on.

The monks return

While her agents burnt bodies to save souls, the Queen herself was troubled in her conscience. It was not the death of heretics which caused her concern, however, but the fact that she and others still held property which in her eyes rightfully belonged to the Church, and that, although the Act of Annates had been repealed, she was still receiving first fruits and tenths. When she broached the matter of restoring annates to the Papacy, men again began to fear that the restoration of the abbey and chantry lands to the Church was not far away, particularly since the Pope had lately published a bull of excommunication against holders of Church lands in other countries. When this bull was being discussed in Council, Lord Bedford became so incensed that he suddenly wrenched his rosary from his belt and slung it into the fire, 'swearing deeply that he loved his sweet abbey of Woburn more than any fatherly counsel or commands that could come from Rome'. Despite the obvious opposition, Mary made it clear that she was determined to get her way, telling her councillors that, even if,

considering the state of the kingdom, and the dignity thereof, my crown imperial cannot be honourably maintained and furnished without the possessions aforesaid; yet notwithstanding, I set more by the salvation of my soul than by ten kingdoms.

The matter of annates was raised in the Parliament which met in October 1555, but all the members would allow the Queen to do was surrender £60,000 a year to the Legate for the augmentation of small livings. She was, of course, free to do what few others cared to – give back the monastic lands she herself held. and that was what she did. English friars had already begun to return from Flanders that spring. Observants were set up at Greenwich, Mary's much-loved birthplace. The Black Friars came home to St Bartholomew's Hospital near the Smithfield execution ground. The Benedictines returned to Westminster, the Bridgettines to Syon, the Carthusians to Sheen. The Dominican canonesses of King's Langley, who had continued to live a community life even after the Dissolution, returned to their old home. By 1557 then, there were six restored houses, containing just over 100 out of the 1,500 religious still alive. In the North Country, the Queen gave several manors back to the Arch-

bishop of York, Nicholas Heath, who, on Gardiner's death in
November 1555, succeeded him as Lord Chancellor. In the same
region, she restored the colleges of clergy at Manchester and
Southwell, and granted lands to the Bishop of Chester.

Plans were afoot in that fourth Parliament of Mary's reign
to bring back from abroad some other Englishmen besides the
exiled friars, namely the authors of the incendiary literature
which was widely circulating in the capital, and those who
intrigued with Spain's enemy the King of France to rid England
of her unwelcome foreign guests. Every Englishman without a
licence to travel was to be summoned home with a promise of
the restoration of confiscated goods if he came, a threat to
confiscate goods not yet impounded if he did not. Realizing that
such a measure could prove ruinous to the Protestant cause,
the exiles' friends in the Commons saw that the bill which contained it was rejected. The Queen's reply was to dissolve Parliament and lock the bill's leading opponents in the Tower.

Catholic reformation

While Parliament had been debating the Queen's business, the
clergy had been meeting in synod to discuss means of proceeding
with God's. The Legate was worried by the indifference and
opposition to organized religion which he saw in the London to
which he had returned. The decaying churches, and the fact that
the once so munificent English now gave less in alms in a year
than just two Italian cities gave in a month caused him considerable anxiety. Like Hooper, he was aware that the chief
obstacle to the conversion of England to any sort of sincere
religion was the lack of able and faithful pastors. He drew up a
plan of campaign for the reform of the clergy which was so
thoroughgoing that it caused the Queen's ambassador to the
Imperial court to declare that 'the more part of the priests of
England would be content he were in Rome again'. He aimed to
get rid of such evils as non-residence, the alienation of Church
lands, the carelessness of bishops in examining ordination candidates, and the self-indulgence, luxury and avarice of priests,

which made them such a poor example to their flocks. Not only that, but he planned to provide a new non-heretical translation of the New Testament, and books of instruction for the faithful. He wished to launch a new attack on heretical books and to see that the traditional ceremonies and ornaments of the Church were everywhere restored. In the spring of 1556 the bishops were sent home to their dioceses to implement that great programme of reform which Pole and his Vatican colleagues had first devised twenty years before. Alas, the obstacles were too great, the man-power too small for much to be done.

The death of an archbishop

Meanwhile, the burning continued. Attempts were made to get the heretics to recant, but sometimes this put the accusers in a pretty predicament. Lawrence Sanders, Rector of All Hallows', Bread Street, said in a reply to the heresy commissioners' charge that he was 'dividing himself by singularity from the Church',

For dividing myself from the Church, I live in the faith wherein I have been brought up since I was fourteen years old; being taught that the power of the Bishop of Rome is but usurped, with many other abuses springing thereof. Yea, this I have received, *even at your hands that are here present*, as a thing agreed upon by the Catholic Church and public authority.

To this there was no answer. There were many young people in England who had never known a time when the English Church had regarded the Pope as anything other than just another foreign bishop, and a reviled one at that.

But the persecution carried on, although only a month after it had begun Renard had told his Imperial master of his fear of a rebellion if it were to do so. Even the dead were not safe. The bodies of Fagius and Bucer were disinterred and burnt, and the remains of Peter Martyr's wife were buried in a dunghill. Bishop Farrar of St David's, an eccentric who pleased neither religious group and was actually in prison at the time of King Edward's death, was condemned by his successor and burnt at Carmarthen.

Bishops Ridley and Latimer appeared before the commission at Oxford, accused of disbelief in transubstantiation and papal authority, Latimer making his position clear in a memorable speech:

I acknowledge a Catholic Church spread throughout the world in which no man may err; without the which unity of the Church no man can be saved; but I know perfectly by God's word that this Church is in all the world and hath not its foundation in Rome only. I acknowledge authority to be given to the spiritualty in matters of religion. I do not deny that in the Sacrament by spirit and grace is the very body and blood of Christ, because that every man by receiving bodily that bread and wine spiritually receiveth the body and blood of Christ, and is made partaker thereby of the merits of Christ's passion.

When he and his companion were taken out to die he spoke some even more memorable words. Exhorting Ridley to 'play the man', he told him they would that day 'light such a candle by God's grace in England as I trust will never be put out'.

The death of an even greater heretic helped to keep that candle burning. This was Thomas Cranmer, the man who had granted that annulment which had brought England and its Queen all their trouble. Although convicted of treason in November 1553, he was still alive in 1556. This was partly because his position of Archbishop meant that authority from Rome was necessary for his sentencing and degrading, and partly because, among other things, his fear of death led him to recant the doctrines for which he was condemned. I say among other things because he was in a real dilemma. He had always maintained the Royal Supremacy in matters ecclesiastical. Indeed he was an Erastian before he was a heretic, and now that the Queen ordered him to acknowledge the papal authority what could he do but accept it, although doing so meant accepting doctrines which his conscience told him were wrong? He was made to sign no less than six submissions to the Holy See – documents which his tormentors, Carranza, Soto and Villagarcia hoped to use as weapons in their holy war against the heretics. At first they were somewhat

ambiguously worded, but eventually he was persuaded to write
this:

Exceedingly offended I against Henry and Catherine in that divorce,
whereof I was the cause and author, which was the seed plot of the
calamities of the realm. Hence the violent death of good men, hence
the schism of the whole kingdom, hence heretics, hence the slaughter
of many souls and bodies . . . I am worse than Saul and the thief,
I am the most wicked wretch that earth has ever borne. I have sinned
against heaven which through me stands empty of so many inhabi-
tants . . . I have sinned against earth, depriving men of the super-
substantial food. Of them that perished for lack of it I am the slayer;
and the souls of the dead I have defrauded of this daily celebrious
sacrifice.

Despite such a thorough and humiliating submission, Cranmer
did not get his reprieve. On 21 March 1556 he was led out from
his Oxford gaol to St Mary's Church to make the public recantation which was to be the prelude to his execution. But, with all
hope of future physical life gone, he decided to make sure of a
spiritual life with his Saviour by saying what he really believed
to be true. Before Cranmer's turn to speak came, Dr Cole, the
Provost of Eton, preached a sermon in which he stated that
Sir Thomas More and Bishop Fisher had been martyred for the
Word of Christ, and that their deaths demanded retribution.
The death of the Duke of Northumberland, a layman, was
retribution for the death of the layman More, and the death of
the cleric Fisher was to be atoned for by the death of the cleric
Cranmer. Then he called on Cranmer to give proof that he died
in the true Faith. The condemned man said the Lord's Prayer,
but to the consternation of his listeners left out the Hail Mary
which he had agreed to say. Then he failed to declare the Queen's
title to the Crown as he was supposed to. However, Cranmer
the Erastian did tell the people to 'obey their King and Queen
willingly and gladly' and bowed the knee as he mentioned their
names. But when the time came for him to make his recantation
this is what he said:

And now I come to that great thing that so much troubleth my
conscience, more than anything that ever I did or said in my whole

life, and that is the setting abroad of a writing contrary to the truth, which now here I renounce and refuse as things written with my hand contrary to the truth which I thought in my heart, and were written for fear of death, and to save my life if it might be; and that is all such bills and papers which I have written or signed with my hand since my degradation, wherein I have written many things untrue. And forasmuch as my hand offended, writing contrary to my heart, my hand shall first be punished therefore: for may I come to the fire it shall first be burned. And as for the Pope, I refuse him as Christ's enemy and Anti-Christ, with all his false doctrine. And as for the Sacrament, I believe as I have taught against the Bishop of Winchester.

With that he was pulled down from the platform and went eagerly out of the church, running to the stake. When the fire was lit, he held his right hand steadily in the flames until he collapsed and died in the fire and smoke. Thus perished the man who had, as much as any other, guided the Church of England through the previous twenty years, providing it with what came to be regarded as its 'incomparable liturgy', with the Forty-two Articles of its Faith, and – almost – with a new legal code. What had been intended as a humiliation for the Protestants turned out to be a triumph. What was supposed to weaken them fortified them, and increased the rapidly growing hatred for the powers responsible for England's orgy of burning. The complete lack of sympathy of a large section of the population for the Government's policy was most clearly manifest when on 29 August a crowd of 1,000 people cheered through the streets a roped chain of twenty-two men and women from Colchester on their way to execution.

Whose responsibility?

Who was responsible for the policy which engendered so much hate that it earned the Queen the eternal epithet 'Bloody Mary'? Most historians of the English Reformation have attempted to apportion blame and they have come to widely differing conclusions. Miss Prescott, Mary's biographer, claims that Bishop

Gardiner, who, according to Renard, was in the spring of 1554 already talking of 'the three . . . bishops [Hooper, Ridley and Latimer], whom he means to have burnt unless they will recant', initiated the policy. Professor Elton says that both Gardiner and Bonner, the bishop of the diocese with the largest number of burnings, went at their persecution with a will, the latter especially displaying 'a coarse liking for the task'. Bonner's apologists, who include Professor Dickens and Mr Crosse, would point out, however, that in London he was so much under the eyes of the Court that he could not evade the task of persecution, and that his diocese, more than the others was a hot-bed of heresy. Miss Prescott feels that the bishops in general cannot bear the whole blame even of carrying out the law as it stood and that some of the blame must go to the laymen who informed against or arrested the victims. She particularly exonerates the chief bishop, Reginald Pole, who, newly priested, succeeded Cranmer as Primate, and whom she sees as a merciful man. Professor Dickens, however, quotes Matthew Parker's description of him as *carnifex et flagellum Ecclesiae Anglicanae*, while Professor Elton brackets him with Mary as the inspiration for the burnings, saying that both of them, though personally kind and inclined to mercy, put principle before expediency and believed that this was the only way in which the souls of Englishmen could be saved from eternal damnation. An examination of the relevant sources has given Professor Dickens the distinct impression that the urge to severity came from the Queen, but some scholars are inclined to wonder how far she was influenced by her husband and the well-qualified heresy hunters he had brought with him. Dr Parker exonerates Philip from blame for the persecution, on the grounds that his father, the Emperor, urged moderation, and that his own chaplain, Castro, preached a sermon in which he said it was better that heretics should live and be converted than that they should die for their sins. Yet both Miss Prescott and Professor Dickens suspect that the sermon was simply a device to divert English attention from the Spanish share in the persecution, Dickens bringing to our notice Philip's later addiction to *autos da fé* and the fact that Spanish historians were later to claim for him the chief praise for the harsh treatment of English heretics. And so the debate continues, though some would regard it as inconclusive and futile.

Whoever was responsible for the burning – the devout Queen, the Council frightened of the disorder which might follow religious dissension, the Queen's husband and his fellow Spaniards, or the bishops – the result is not in doubt. Although judicial death by burning was not altogether unusual, and burning for heresy took place on a much larger scale on the Continent, things had never been like this in England before. Those who saw their neighbours and friends taken for trial or tied to the stake felt an intense hostility towards those powers who in any way bore responsibility for what was happening. And the memory of what had happened long outlived the Queen in whose reign it was inspired. Along with the plots and Armada of the next reign, it helped to create an English loathing for Rome and all it stood for, and an intense religious bigotry which even yet is not completely dead.

Unpopularity and death

How miserable Mary's last years must have been! Deserted by her husband, disappointed in her hopes for a child, blamed for the persecution, she was to see her kingdom in a state of war with the Holy Father of Rome. One of Philip's aims in marrying Mary – some would say his only aim – was to bring England into the Hapsburg alliance. And he was in particular need of England's help in the latter months of 1556, when he was faced with opposition from both France and the Holy See. The Pope, Paul IV, was a Neapolitan who hated the Spanish occupation of his country and was determined to end it. Philip sent troops against the Papal States to deal the first blow, and Henry of France announced that he would regard any attack on the Pope, his ally, as an attack on himself and, under the influence of the warlike Guise faction, had no option but to join in hostilities. Paul acted against England as though she were already at one with Spain. Recalling his legates from all the Spanish dominions he also recalled Pole to answer 'some religious suspicions'. In other words the Cardinal was to be tried for heresy. The charge was obviously an unfounded one, and the wily old Pope was simply using Pole's tendencies to Catholic reform as a handle against him, and indirectly against Philip. The Queen, notified in advance of what was happening, ordered that the Papal Nuncio bearing Pole's summons to Rome should be held up at Calais so that the letters of recall should not be received in England, and therefore not disobeyed. What is more, she re-asserted England's traditional freedom of interference from the Holy See by informing the Pope that if charges were to be laid against the Cardinal for heresy, 'she would, in observance of the laws and privileges of her realm, refer them to the cognizance and decision of her own ecclesiastical courts'. However, Paul continued with his game, appointing as Pole's successor an old friar, Cardinal Peto, whom the English ambassador to Rome, Sir Edward Carne, described as a 'blockhead' and 'an old dotard who could not bear any fatigue but merely stay in his cell reciting orisons'. When Carne protested against the change, the reply he received was that the Pope needed Pole's counsel at Rome. Friar Peto actually refused the legatine office, and Carne was instructed that, should the Pope give a flat denial of the Queen's request that Pole should remain as legate, he was to make a further protest and leave Rome. The links Mary and the Cardinal had worked so hard to forge seemed to be quickly wearing away.

Meanwhile Henry II had found a weapon to use against England in the person of Pole's nephew, Henry Stafford, who put forward a claim to Mary's throne. His attempt to take the crown was a farce, but it persuaded the Council into giving way to Philip's pressure and agreeing that England should throw in her lot with him against France. The result of this involvement in continental strife was what every schoolboy knows – the loss of Calais. Though, looked at rationally, this was perhaps more of a blessing than a disaster and, though there was some reason to believe that the town was lost through the treachery of some members of its garrison, it led to a further diminution in the

Queen's popularity. It also led to a reduction in interest in the Queen's brand of religion. The Spanish ambassador wrote:

I am told that, since the loss of Calais, not a third of the people who usually go to church are now attending.

Mary for her part continued to help the Church she loved. A large number of Crown livings were handed over to the bishops so that they could find suitable incumbents for them, and men who agreed with her religious views were appointed to important judicial and administrative posts. But time was running out. Her hope of a son and heir was once again disappointed; the Spanish marriage, the religious persecution, the loss of Calais had turned her people's love for her into hate. She lost the will to live. Early in the morning of 17 November 1558 her tragic life came to its close. Her Archbishop and counsellor died a few hours later.

Further Reading

There are comparatively few books on the reign of Mary. A brief survey of the reign can be found in that deservedly popular little book, S. T. Bindoff, *Tudor England* (Penguin, 1950). The best biography of the Queen is probably H. F. M. Prescott, *Mary Tudor* (Eyre and Spottiswoode, 1952). Her adviser and archbishop is quite adequately treated in Frederic Schenk, *Reginald Pole; cardinal of England* (Longmans, 1950).

For the effects of the religious changes in particular parts of the country see A. G. Dickens, *The Marian Reaction in the Diocese of York* (St Antony's Hall Publications XI–XII, 1957), and James E. Oxley, *The Reformation in Essex to the death of Mary* (Manchester University Press, 1965). Wyatt's Rebellion is dealt with in Mr Fletcher's book. Details of the religious refugees are given in that well-researched work, Christina M. Garret, *The Marian Exiles: a Study in the Origins of Elizabethan Puritanism* (Cambridge University Press, 1938), but the author's personal observations have been much criticized. There are short biographies of the martyrs, Latimer, Ridley and Cranmer in Marcus L. Loane, *Masters of the Reformation* (Church Book Room Press, 1954). The best full-length biography of

Cranmer is generally agreed to be Jasper Ridley, *Thomas Cranmer* (Oxford Paperbacks, 1966), though F. E. Hutchinson, *Cranmer and the English Reformation* (English Universities Press, 1951) is also interesting. Harold S. Darby's *Hugh Latimer* (Epworth Press, 1953), and J. G. Ridley's *Nicholas Ridley: A Biography* (Longmans, 1957) also merit examination, while the effect of their persecution on public opinion is examined in D. M. Loades, *The Oxford Martyrs* (Batsford, 1970).

Principal Events

1553. Queen Mary succeeds to the throne. Gardiner, Lord
   Chancellor. Cranmer, Latimer and Ridley imprisoned. Many
   of the reformers flee.
   First Parliament (October–December) declares 'divorce' of
   Queen's parents unlawful and establishes her legitimacy.
   Laws of Edward VI's reign relating to religion repealed. The
   services of the Church ordered to be those commonly used in
   the last year of Henry VIII
1554. Second Parliament (April–May). Convocation also summoned;
   deputes a commission to argue with Cranmer, Ridley and
   Latimer; condemns them as heretics. Wyatt's rebellion.
   Marriage of Queen to Philip of Spain (July). The bishops visit
   their dioceses. Some of the clergy deprived for marriage.
   Third Parliament (November–January). Pole enters England
   as Legate (24 November). England reconciled with Rome.
   Parliament repeals all Acts against the Pope's authority since
   1529; only the present possessors of Church lands are secured.
   Act restoring heresy laws. Pole tries to effect a reformation
   of the clergy
1555. Persecution begins. Rogers, Hooper, Ridley, Latimer and
   others burnt. Fourth Parliament (October–December).
   Failure of move to restore annates to Papacy
1556. Cranmer burnt. Pole made Archbishop of Canterbury
1557. England involved by Philip in war with France. Pole accused
   of heresy
1558. Fifth Parliament (January–November). Loss of Calais
   (January). Death of the Queen (17 November). Pole dies
   the next day

PART VI
The Church in 1558

[13] THE NEW QUEEN

Her character

On the day Queen Mary died history repeated itself, the scenes in her capital ironically echoing those of five years before when she had entered the city in triumph, the most welcome symbol of the collapse of Northumberland's régime. In diarist's words.

All the churches in London did ring, and at night [men] did make bonfires and set tables in the street, and did eat and drink and made merry for the new queen.

People rejoiced because they were glad to be rid of the Spanish Tudor and hoped that their bonfires signalled the end of the awful fires of death lit by her religious zeal. They had a new Queen who rejoiced to be 'mere English', a Queen so like her father – intelligent and learned, and, as the Spanish ambassador recorded, 'much attached to the people' and 'very confident that they are all on her side, which is indeed true'. The same witness tells us something more of Elizabeth's similarity to her father, which was physical as well as intellectual:

She seems to me incomparably more feared than her sister, and gives orders and has her way as absolutely as her father did.

Perhaps the young woman of twenty-five who now sat on the English throne had inherited something of this art of getting her way with men from her mother. Anne Boleyn's daughter was ever a deceiver. She could say one thing and believe another and not turn a hair. The art of deception had helped her survive some very difficult, indeed dangerous situations, and was to get her through many more. 'With her', wrote another Spanish envoy, 'all is falsehood and vanity.'

Her religion and her early life

In her sister's reign Elizabeth had needed all her native wit and womanly arts to keep both her life and her title to the succession. Labelled a bastard by her father, her illegitimacy had not been erased by Act of Parliament at the same time as Mary's, and the late Queen had on several occasions attempted to deprive her of her right to succeed. Her religion was both her strength and her weakness. It made her the heroine of those who detested the official religious policy, and caused those responsible for its implementation to regard her with grave suspicion.

The offspring of the liaison which had helped bring about the break with Rome, she had never till her sister's reign known a papist England. Her tutors were of the same Cambridge school as those of her brother, Edward VI. She had been much attached to her step-mother, Catherine Parr, and had, for a short while after her father's death, lived in the Protestant atmosphere of the Queen Dowager's household. She had conformed under Somerset and Northumberland, but when Mary succeeded and Mass was said at court Elizabeth kept away. However, in those early days the Queen was popular, and to defy her was dangerous. Younger sister thought it politic to give way to elder. Turning on the tears, she begged for books or teachers to mend the error of her ways, and she attended Mass. However, she went infrequently enough to let her Protestant friends know that she was not as devout as the Queen would have liked to believe. Mary herself soon began to have her doubts but, when she questioned Elizabeth on the genuineness of her conversion, the latter assured her that it was the dictate of conscience and told her that she was thinking of making a public declaration to that effect. Yet she was surrounded by ladies-in-waiting who were all heretics, there is little doubt that she was connected with Wyatt's plot, and several members of her household were proved to be in league with the emigrés who plotted with the French to overthrow the Government. Despite the weight of evidence against her, she survived. She won Philip's friendship and perhaps his heart. He hoped that, if Mary were to die without giving birth, as seemed likely, Elizabeth, as her successor, would pursue a pro-Spanish policy, and felt bound to defend her against her enemies. And, as Mary's star fell, Elizabeth's rose. When, at the time of the French threat, her London house was searched and a great coffer was found full of seditious, Protestant books and broadsheets, no strong action could be risked because of her growing popularity. For people of all shades of religious and political opinion the only possible alternative to Mary as Queen was the other daughter of Henry VIII. There were other claimants, but reaction to the events of Mary's reign had made it inevitable that when the one sister died the other should succeed. At last Mary had to perform a task she had long shown reluctance for – recognize Elizabeth as her successor. She did so on 6 November 1558, coupling the recognition with a vain request that she would retain the link with Rome.

[14] THE STATE OF RELIGION IN ENGLAND

A backward glance

The religious situation which Elizabeth inherited was, to say the least, a difficult one. Almost thirty years had passed since the first meeting of the Reformation Parliament. In those thirty years a great deal had happened. The English Church in 1558 might have stood in a similar relationship to Sovereign and to Pope as it had in 1529, but the problems which it had to handle were much more complex. The Faith it taught was the same, but the enemies of that Faith were different, more numerous and infinitely stronger. Once it had had to withstand the assaults of a few thousand artisans and country bumpkins, for the most part incapable of an intellectual defence of the garbled creed handed on to them through a century and a half of disorganized dissent, and of a few university-trained loyalists whose chief object for attack was not doctrine but indiscipline. In the 1520s and 1530s it was faced by a new and disciplined enemy, with commanders who were the living inspiration of the war of words its troops conducted, and a new and powerful weapon – the printing press. The King, perhaps to some extent inspired by the action of his fellow princes in Germany as well as the demands of nation, heart and conscience, broke with the Holy See, and found himself forced to accept allies who were themselves tainted with the new continental heresy. The hierarchy came to be divided into conservatives and radicals; the voice and power of the Church was weakened further by the destruction of its religious houses and the secularization of its property; its activities were restricted by King and Parliament. Once entrenched in Court and cathedral, heresy spread rapidly, at times being helped along by the dictates of foreign policy. At last the Government fell into the hands of a man who combined zeal for reform with personal greed. The Church lost more of its wealth and its independence, its traditional rites and ceremonies were pruned, and its reforming Archbishop was given the freedom he sought to make England into a reformers' Mecca. Protestantism more radical than that of the 1520s and 1530s pushed down deep roots in the England of the late 1540s and early 1550s. The universities, once the strongholds of Lutheranism, were now the nurseries of the Swiss heresies. The priesthood was stripped of its trappings; it no longer offered its Saviour as a sacrifice for the living and the dead; it ceased to loose and bind in the confessional. Its members were no longer men set apart to handle the sacramental mysteries. For many, celibacy gave way to family; all were ordered to set the preaching of the Word above the administration of the Sacraments. A nation, many of whose people had already been persuaded into anti-clericalism by the interference and exactions of a rich and unworldly Church, and which had already begun to criticize its ministers in the light of a Gospel all were now free to read, had become divided in matters of faith. Two rebellions, one in the west of the country and one in the east, demonstrated how far England was two nations spiritually. And when a new reign began and an attempt was made to turn back the clock, it soon became apparent how strong the new Faith was, how deep its roots. Rejected by the Government which had once nurtured it, it sought and found succour in the Continent which had given it birth; at home it was fortified by a baptism of fire.

1558

While the bishops of the Church were being subjected to attacks from abroad and – impossible task – tried to stamp out heresy at home, its lesser ministers continued to tend their flocks, or to neglect them, in just the same way that they had thirty years before. Much had changed, but much remained the same. The need for reform had been all but forgotten amidst the theological and political strife of the so-called Reformation. Much of what Colet and Erasmus had criticized in the early years of the century was still a conspicuous feature of Church life in the 1550s, and was to remain so for the rest of the century. Nay, for far longer than that. Some of the same scandals and abuses were still there for Wesley to struggle against in the eighteenth century and for the several Church movements of the nineteenth century to combat. Indeed the Church of today would scarcely show up in a very good light if it were judged by the standards of the Pauline theologians of four and a half centuries ago.

Bishops like Hooper and Pole who made a sincere and genuine effort to rid the Church of its abuses were all too few, and it is not unlikely that while the wrangling went on in high places abuses grew rather than diminished at parish level. Some clergy were rich, others still very poor and growing poorer as the cost of living rose. An Act of 1549 had exempted several classes of tithe-payers and made tithes more difficult to collect. And in the towns it was so difficult to assess wealth arising out of trade or industry for tithing, that how much or how little was given depended on the individual conscience. Then the gentry who had replaced the monks as proprietors of benefices were often very mean when it came to paying stipends. As lay-Rectors they kept the greater tithes for themselves and gave nothing to the

Church in return. The problem of inequality among the parish
clergy is one which is still unresolved. In the 1550s, pluralism
and non-residence were still rife; some churches, deprived of
their married priests were inadequately served. In many places,
but particularly in London, church fabrics fell into ruin. Chancels
were neglected by lay-Rectors and ill-paid priests, naves by
parishioners who, having seen a lifetime's treasured ornaments
swept away in King Edward's time, were unsure whether further
expenditure would be worthwhile, or who were simply indifferent.
In some places where devotion still flourished, roods and statues
were beginning to reappear; in others no one cared enough to
effect a few repairs. Cardinal Pole had complained that, unlike
the monasteries which had been pulled down, parish churches
had been 'suffered to fall down of themselves'. Elizabeth's
Bishop Jewel was to record sorrowfully, 'It is a sin and a shame
to see so many churches ruinous and so foully decayed'.

Churchwardens had much more to do than look after the
churches. They had charge of social security, though Elizabeth
was to transfer the care of the poor to overseers selected by the
magistrates. They had also to provide arms for the local militia
and maintain roads and bridges, stocks and whipping post.
They still held church ales, rented out the church house and kept
livestock. Parochial duty kept laymen in close touch with their
clergy, and sometimes made the poor standard of literacy among
the priesthood only too apparent. In 1560, in the diocese of
Winchester only 19 per cent of the clergy were university graduates; even in the diocese of Oxford, with its large band of university teachers, only 38 per cent were graduates.

Secularism was growing. Laymen, with scant respect for their
clergy and tired of doctrinal argument, had become increasingly
indifferent to religion. If they wanted to perform some charitable
or educational good work they no longer did it through the
agency of the Church. The fate of the chantries had in any case
shown what was likely to happen to bequests made for ecclesiastical purposes. Charity did not diminish but, outside conservative
areas, it was inspired by the family Bible and individual conscience, rather than the parish priest and general exhortation.

Despite the growth of secularism, despite the curtailment of the Church's rights and the confiscation of its wealth in the past thirty years, the clergy retained and were to retain, a number of their ancient privileges. Their courts still sat in judgment over laymen accused of moral lapses, and inflicted on them the indignity of a public penance, while they themselves could make the consequences of their crimes less severe than they might have been by claiming, as they did till 1827, benefit of clergy.

The Church of 1558 was poorer both materially and influentially than that of 1529, yet its personnel were still privileged and, in theory, all English people were still its members. That those members did not all agree with its teaching, indeed that some abhorred it as the teaching of Anti-Christ, presented the new Queen's Government, as anxious as any to keep the people united and avoid civil strife, with very great problems.

The way ahead

That the Church should continue to be subject to Rome was not a practicable possibility. Elizabeth's own religious leanings, the nature of her staunchest support, the expectations of her most loyal subjects ruled this out. In the first official document of her reign she used, for other reasons than her sister's, the vague, but tell-tale 'etc.' to conclude her titles. Yet she had at first to play her cards extremely carefully. By the canon law of the universal Church and the statute law of England, she was illegitimate. Across the Channel in France was a legitimate claimant to the throne – Mary Stuart, the wife of the Dauphin – and papal support for her claim was far from an impossibility. Her country still officially at war with France, Elizabeth needed the support of Spain. Philip was unlikely to tolerate the expansion of French power through the conquest of England, but he was equally unlikely to view with equanimity an attack on his Faith. The new Queen wanted time to establish herself firmly on her throne, and could not risk trouble either from the European powers or from the conservative hierarchy at home. Although there was no longer a formal embassy to the Holy See an agent was retained at Rome, and Elizabeth promised to restore full diplomatic relations. And Mass continued to be said in the royal chapel.

However, exiles were returning in their droves from the Continent, expecting their heroine Queen to be in the van of the movement for the reformation and purification of the Church. Bullinger and Peter Martyr wrote to salute her on her accession. 'Now', said the exiles, 'is the time for the walls of Jerusalem to be built again in that kingdom, that the blood of so many martyrs, so largely shed, may not be in vain.' Bishop White of Winchester had a different notion of what religious change meant:

The wolves be coming out of Geneva and other places of Germany, and hath sent their books before, full of pestilent doctrines, blasphemy, and heresy to infect the people.

Those imprisoned for heresy under Mary were let out of gaol, and heretic congregations began to hold their still illegal Prayer Book services in public. By Christmas the esteem in which she was held by her people had given Elizabeth enough confidence for her to give some indication of where she herself stood in matters of faith. She ordered the Bishop of Carlisle, who was celebrating Mass in her chapel, not to make the customary act of sacrifice, the elevation of the Host. Since he refused to obey, she walked out immediately after the reading of the Gospel. Two days later a proclamation was issued which, by introducing a modicum of English into the liturgy, seemed to suggest a return to the situation at her father's death. Since the Government – eleven councillors had served under Mary: seven were moderate Protestants like William Cecil – were concerned at the possibility of national disunity being one of the consequences of the return of the 'wolves' and of open nonconformist worship, it also in a sense echoed the proclamations and Acts of Parliament of the previous three reigns:

The Queen's Majesty understanding that there be certain persons having in times past the office of ministry in the Church, which do now purpose to use their former office in preaching and ministry, and partly have attempted the same, assembling specially in the city of London, in sundry places, great number of people; whereupon riseth among the common sort not only unfruitful disputes in matters of religion, but also contention and occasion to break common quiet; hath therefore according to the authority committed to her Highness, for the quiet governance of all manner of her subjects, thought it necessary to charge and command, like as hereby her Highness doth charge and command, all manner of her subjects, as well those as be called to ministry in the Church as all others: that they do forbear to preach or teach, or to give audience to any manner of doctrine or preaching, other than to the Gospels and Epistles commonly called the Gospel and Epistle of the day, and to the Ten Commandments in the vulgar tongue, without exposition or addition of any manner sense or meaning to be applied and added; or to use any manner of public prayer, rite or ceremony in the Church, but that which is already used and by law received, as the Common Litany used at this present in Her Majesty's Chapel, and the Lord's Prayer and the Creed in English; until consultation may be had by Parliament by Her Majesty, and her three estates of this realm, for the better conciliation and accord of such causes as at this present are moved in matters and ceremonies of religion.

What was needed but difficult to achieve was some sort of compromise religious settlement which would please the majority of the people and prevent the civil strife which was so much feared. Elizabeth, however, told the Spanish ambassador that she was resolved to restore religion as her father had left it; but then diplomatic necessity caused her to give different accounts of her personal faith to the representatives of different countries, Lutheran, Calvinist or Catholic. However, Professor Owen Chadwick believes that her ideas of a religious settlement included the Royal Supremacy, Catholicism without the Pope, a preferably celibate clergy, and the Real Presence in the Eucharist. When, some years later, she told another Spaniard that the Protestants had driven her further than she had intended to go, he feels she was speaking the truth. Professor Dickens, pointing to such evidence as the choice of William Bill, a noted Protestant, to be her first preacher at Paul's Cross and the imprisonment of a bishop who criticized his sermon, says that she intended from the first to figure in the character of a Protestant monarch. He finds it almost impossible to believe that at any stage she contemplated a return to 'her father's brand of orthodoxy'.

It does seem, however, that the Queen intended to proceed
with caution, and, if such was her plan, to reverse the Marian
settlement at almost as leisurely a rate as it had been made.
When Parliament met early in 1559, a bill was introduced to
restore the Royal Supremacy. It also embodied a section allowing the laity Communion in both kinds, and that seems to have
been the only liturgical reform intended at the time. However,
there was strong opposition to the bill from the Marian bishops
in both Lords and Convocation. These men, unlike the Henrician
bishops, who had themselves only reluctantly accepted the
Royal Supremacy, had been appointed to their sees not simply
because of their loyalty and service to the Crown, but because
of their wholehearted support for the link with Rome. A few, it
is true, had served under Henry but they had not liked the way
the Royal Supremacy had taken them under his son. It soon
became evident that they would be likely to refuse to take an
oath of Supremacy if such were tendered to them. With ten
sees already vacant through death, it seemed inevitable that an
almost complete new hierarchy would have to be found from
somewhere. Many of the really able clerics were numbered among
the exiles and nonconformists of Mary's reign, and it seemed that
the new bishops would have to come from that source, particularly since they would be more ready than the clergymen
already holding high office in the Church to accept the Royal
Supremacy. Apparently in view of the need to please the likely
candidates for the episcopal purple, of vociferous opposition
to the Supremacy Bill as it stood from a strong Protestant element in the Commons, and perhaps of news that peace was
about to be made with France, thus alleviating the danger from
abroad, the Government appears suddenly to have changed its
plans. Professor Dickens feels that it was trying to effect a
compromise between those upholders of Catholic orthodoxy
who were willing to reject the Pope and those radicals of the
Coxian school who adhered to the English Prayer Book, and that
the basis for that compromise was to be joint acceptance of the
1549 liturgy. Cox's party would, however, accept nothing more
conservative than the 1552 rite. Accordingly a Bill of Uniformity

was put through Parliament enforcing the use of the 1552 book with one or two significant 'compromise' modifications. A rubric which soon became a dead letter declared that the ornaments of the churches and their ministers should be those of the second year of Edward's reign, a time when coloured vestments were still worn and churches were still furnished in much the same way as in pre-Reformation days. The Black Rubric of 1552, which said that no adoration was implied by kneeling to receive Communion, was omitted. And the words of administration of 1552 were to be preceded by those of 1549; the priest saying to each communicant,

The Body of our Lord Jesus Christ which was given for thee, preserve thy body and soul unto everlasting life. Take and eat this in remembrance that Christ died for thee, and feed on him in thy heart by faith, with thanksgiving.

The communicant was free to interpret these words in whatever way he would. Another change was the omission from the Litany of the offensive reference to the Pope and his 'detestable enormities'. Then by the new Act of Supremacy, the Queen took a compromise title – that of 'Supreme Governor' of the Church, 'Supreme Head' being distasteful on different grounds to conservative and radical alike. Professor Bindoff says that the new formula mollified both Philip II, who regarded the Pope as the only head of the Church on earth, and zealous Calvinists, some of whom objected most strongly to such a title being held by a woman, St Paul having said that women should be silent in church. In effect the new title gave its holder the same power as the old, Elizabeth disciplining her clergy by means of a powerful new Court of High Commission which sat in her name.

The new religious settlement brought in its wake change and disorder not unlike that already witnessed in earlier reigns. Only two bishops, Kitchin of Llandaff and Stanley of Man, took the Oath of Supremacy, and the rest were deprived. One or two managed to escape abroad, like the monks and nuns whose conventual life in England again came to an end; the others

were kept in what was sometimes a not too close confinement.
The vacancies were filled by former exiles such as Cox and Jewel,
and by more moderate radicals who had stayed at home but
managed to evade persecution, like Matthew Parker, who
succeeded Pole as Primate. Not all the new diocesans were
complete newcomers to the episcopal bench. William Barlow,
the Henrician Bishop of St David's and Edwardian Bishop of
Bath and Wells, was appointed to the see of Chichester, and
John Scory, who had been at Chichester in King Edward's
day, was sent to Hereford. And the episcopacy reflected quite a
wide spectrum of beliefs. If Parker was more moderate than
Cox, Cheney of Bristol was even more so. In fact the people of
Bristol complained to Cecil about his teaching of the Real
Presence and his belief in free will as opposed to predestination,
doctrines which led him to protest when a revised form of the
Forty-two Articles, the Thirty-nine Articles, was adopted as the
English Church's official statement of its Faith. He made no
secret of his fondness for pictures and crucifixes in churches,
and was thought a likely convert by the agents of the Holy See.

The mass of the clergy took the oath, being anxious to keep
their livelihoods and perhaps not aware of how radically things
were going to change. Indeed, some thought that the changes
would, like those of Edward's reign, be short-lived. Many would
be pleased to have their wives and families back with them
again. The ex-monks continued to draw their pensions and their
stipends. Higher dignitaries, more obviously aware than the
poorly educated parish priests of what the changes in faith and
order really meant, stayed at the posts they had held without a
break from King Henry's time. Nicholas Wotton, who had
served the Queen's father, brother and sister as Dean of Canterbury and Dean of York, continued to hold both offices and to
draw their fat stipends. Dr Perne, the Master of Peterhouse, who
had been Vice-Chancellor of Cambridge University at the time
when Bucer's and Fagius's corpses were burnt in the market
place, was still Master and again Vice-Chancellor when the
Senate unanimously agreed to restore their degrees to them and
a public service was held in their honour.

Undoubtedly some clergy were reluctant to take the oath and others did so with tongue in cheek (Bishop Best of Carlisle called his priests 'wicked imps of Anti-Christ', and Scory thought his clergy 'dissemblers and rank Papists'). Estimates of the number who were deprived vary, but the latest puts it at not more than 200, less than 4 per cent of the total clerical body. There were candidates for the vacancies they left: viz. the formerly deprived married priests who were now free to seek office again. However, there were still livings to fill and, till enough new ministers were ordained, in some places specially appointed lay-readers, usually of little education and sometimes of bad character, and in others the parish clerks said divine service, baptized, and solemnized matrimony. When a priest was present, the clerk had the right to read the Epistle and administer the chalice to the laity at the Holy Communion, to read the lessons at Morning and Evening Prayer, and to lead the people in that new feature of Anglican worship – the metrical psalm. Although for a time considerable reliance was laid on a sometimes not very impressive lay ministry, in at least one respect the quality of the pastorate improved. Everywhere the proportion of graduates in the priesthood grew.

However, some old scandals continued and others gave way to new. An unofficial survey of the clergy made in 1584 revealed that there was a fair proportion of drunkards and adulterers in their ranks. The sons of the vicarage often became vicars themselves, and some livings tended to be handed down almost as if they were real estate. The legitimate children of the more influential of the Elizabethan clergy sometimes were given benefices when still minors, in the same way that their illegitimate Henrician counterparts had been. Younger sons of squires got livings in their fathers' patronage; ministers were appointed whose theological tendencies were those of the patron. And those who gained bishoprics were still in general, though not entirely without exception, the Sovereign's men. They were now more generally pastors than courtiers, and seldom held high office under the Crown, but they retained a number of secular duties, often serving as local magistrates. Then, the Queen,

like her father and even more like her brother's guardian, tended
to regard her bishops' property as her own. She kept some sees
vacant for years in order to take their income for herself, and
she robbed others of their estates. Bishop Cox once said that it
would not do for the Queen to learn 'how great a grazier, how
marvellous a dairyman, how rich a farmer' he was, but even if
he tried to keep it a secret she found out, and in the end he resigned in vexation at the terrible despoliation of his see.

A large section of the laity were annoyed by a different kind
of despoliation. The commissioners sent round to tender the
Supremacy Oath were also ordered to deliver some new injunctions to the clergy. One was directed against shrines, images and
'monuments of feigned miracles, pilgrimages, idolatry and superstition'. In some places the offending images were destroyed.
In the church-wardens' accounts of a Somerset parish for 1559–60
we find the following entries:

For taking down the rood	vd
In expenses for the plucking down of the images	vid
For taking down the altar	iis

Walls were whitewashed once again, and, although the injunctions did not require it, stone altars were again replaced with
wooden tables. An eyewitness commented:

As for our churches, bells and times of morning and evening prayer
remain as in times past, saving that all images, shrines, tabernacles,
rood-lofts, and monuments of idolatry are removed, taken down and
defaced, only the stories in glass windows excepted, which, for want
of sufficient store of new stuff, and by reason of extreme charge that
should grow by the alteration of the same into white panes throughout the realm, are not altogether abolished in most places at once,
but by little and little suffered to decay, that white glass may be
provided and set up in their rooms.

This picture might have been true of some parts of the country
within a few months of the injunctions being issued, but it was
certainly not true of some of the remoter and more conservative
parts of the kingdom, nor indeed of some places not far removed
from the capital. In 1562 a new Book of Homilies was published

for reading in churches and one of the sermons contained therein
was an attack on idolatry by Bishop Jewel. In it he wrote,

our churches stand full of such great puppets, wondrously decked
and adorned; garlands and coronets be set on their heads, precious
stones hanging about their necks; their fingers shine with rings set
with precious stones; their dead and stiff bodies are clothed with
garments stiff with gold.

Some members of the new, radical hierarchy were distressed by
the appearance of the royal chapel. In 1563, Bishop Parkhurst
of Norwich wrote,

the cross, wax candles and candlesticks had been removed from the
queen's chapel; but they were shortly after brought back again, to the
great grief of the godly . . . The lukewarmness of some persons very
much retards the progress of the gospel.

As late as 1569, Archbishop Parker investigated the situation
in the diocese of Chichester and reported that

In some places because the Rood was taken away, they painted in
that place a cross with chalk, and because that was washed away
with painting and the number of crosses standing at graves in the
churchyard taken also away, they have since made crosses on the
church walls within and without, and upon the pulpit and Communion Table in despite of the preacher . . . In some places the rood
lofts still stand, and those taken down still lie in the churches ready
to be put up again.

'Ready to be put up again' – a significant phrase. Many
expected the change in religion to be as short-lived as that of
Edward's reign. Again churches put away their vestments –
banned by radically minded bishops despite the ornaments
rubric – in the hope that they would one day be used again.
And, although parishes bought new cups with which to communicate the laity, some kept the chalices from which only the
priest had drunk in days gone by. When Philip Baker, the Provost
of King's College, Cambridge, was accused in 1565 of hoarding
missals, pyxes, vestments, etc., and ordered to destroy them,
he refused, saying, 'That which hath been may be again'.

In 1571, Archbishop Grindal, Parker's successor still found it necessary to issue injunctions ordering the destruction of altars and rood lofts, and indeed to forbid such practices as making the sign of the cross on entering church, telling beads, and burning candles in church on Candlemas Day. Four years later he issued visitation interrogatories which echoed Bishop Ridley's injunctions of more than a quarter of a century before, asking

Whether your parson, vicar, curate, or minister do wear any cope in your parish church or chapel, or minister the holy Communion in any chalice heretofore used at mass, or in any profane cup or glass, or use at the ministration thereof any gestures, rites or ceremonies, not appointed by the book of Common Prayer, as crossing or breathing over the sacramental bread and wine, or shewing the same to the people to be worshipped and adored, or any such like, or use any oil and chrism, tapers, spattle, or any other popish ceremony in the administration of the sacrament of Baptism?

Even those clergy who conformed were suspect. In 1571, John Northbrook, in his work, *A Brief and Pithy Sum of the Christian Faith*, wrote of ministers who

draw nigh with tongue and pen unto us, but their hearts are at Rome. A number of them have gospel talk, but yet a Romish faith; an English face, but Spanish hearts . . . For they think now that if they subscribe, observe the order of service and wear a silk gown, a square cap, a cope and a surplice . . . they are good Protestants: yet all this while they run hugger mugger, a-whispering in corners, saying to simple people, 'Believe not this new doctrine; it will not endure. Although I use order among them outwardly, my heart and profession is from them, agreeing with the mother Church of Rome. No, no (they say) we do not preach nor yet teach openly. We read their new devised homilies for a colour, to satisfy them for a season.

But the time hoped for never came. There were priests who would on the same day celebrate the Holy Communion in church according to the Prayer Book rite, and the old Mass in the house of a parishioner. Some even delivered Hosts consecrated after the old fashion to communicants kneeling in church alongside other parishioners who received Communion in both kinds according to the new. But, as the years went by, priests brought up in the old tradition became fewer and fewer. There came a time when the vast majority of the clergy were ministers of the Gospel who knew no theology but the Swiss and said no liturgy but that of the Book of Common Prayer, and those who clung to the old ways had to seek ministrations from elsewhere. In 1563, the Pope, despairing of the English Church again accepting his authority, decreed that those Englishmen who attended their parish services fell into the sin of schism; in 1570 he excommunicated and deposed the Queen; in 1573 priests who had been trained at a college set up by English exiles at Douai in the Netherlands began to enter the country, and they were followed by the black-habited soldiers of the Counter-Reformation, the Jesuits. It has been estimated, but perhaps with some exaggeration, that by 1583 there were about 120,000 men, women and children in England who could be properly described as Roman Catholics. The aim of Tudor governments to maintain the unity of the English Church despite diversities of religious belief had failed, and, as had happened in Mary's reign, persecution was to strengthen, rather than weaken, the dissidents. Dissent increased as the bishops tried to make Puritans more radical than themselves conform, and such features of the Elizabethan Church and its ritual as vestments, the sign of the cross in Baptism, and the giving of the wedding ring, gave way to episcopacy itself as the object of attack. It was not until the next century that recognizable non-Anglican Protestant Churches existed in this country at anything more than a local level, but the seeds were already being sown in the Separatist congregations of the South-East. To all the scandals which already existed in the religious life of England was added a greater one – the scandal of disunity. Nonconformity was not new: the existence of organized churches in hostile opposition to one another was. Such was the legacy of the English Reformation.

Further Reading

The story told here is continued in another volume in this series, H. G. Alexander, *Religion in England 1558–1662* (University of

London Press, 1968). To the excellent bibliographies contained in that book I would add Sir John Neale's famous biography of the last Tudor monarch, *Queen Elizabeth I* (Penguin, 1960), Claire Cross, *The Royal Supremacy in the Elizabethan Church* (Allen and Unwin, 1969) and the following works which deal with the transitional period during which the old ornaments and ancient ceremonies continued in the parish churches despite the opposition of a largely Calvinist hierarchy: A. H. Dodd, *Life in Elizabethan England* (Batsford, 1961), particularly interesting for its account of the situation in Wales; M. D. R. Leys, *Catholics in England 1559–1829 – A Social History* (Longmans, 1961); and A. Tindal Hart, *The Man in the Pew 1558–1660* (John Baker, 1966). Extracts from documents relating to this period are given in that fascinating work edited by Father Philip Caraman, *The Other Face, Catholic Life under Elizabeth I* (Longmans, 1960).

The English Reformation can only be properly understood against its political background and in the light of what was going on at the time on the Continent of Europe. The standard works on events at home are in the 'Oxford History of England' series: J. D. Mackie, *The Earlier Tudors 1485–1558* (Oxford University Press, 1952) and J. B. Black, *The Reign of Elizabeth* (Oxford University Press, second edition, 1959), but they are now very dated. However, Conrad Russell makes use of much recent research in his *The Crisis of Parliaments, English History 1509–1660* (Oxford University Press, 1971), and Mrs Margaret Bowker is preparing a general account of the period which will be published as a Sphere paperback. G. R. Elton, *England under the Tudors* (Methuen, 1955) is a very popular book, but should be treated with caution where matters of religion are concerned, for it is in some need of revision in the light of recent research and current opinion. I have no hesitation, however, in recommending the same author's *Reformation Europe, 1517–1559* (Collins/Fontana, 1963) as an introduction to events on the Continent. A newer book which tells the same story very simply, by means of quotations from original sources, is Leonard W. Cowie, *The Reformation of the Sixteenth Century* (Wayland Publishers, 1970).

In preparing the bibliographies for this book, I have confined myself to books at present in print, but the writing of the history of the Reformation is an activity as old as the Reformation itself. All serious students of the subject should gain an acquaintanceship with that pioneer work of historical scholarship and modern research technique, Foxe's *Acts and Monuments*, with the brilliantly written royal biographies by J. A. Froude, and the histories of the English Church by Dixon, Gairdner and Frere. They reflect (Frere less so than the others) somewhat out-dated partisan approaches to the study of the subject, but help the student to understand how ideas on the English Reformation have developed, to recognize bias, and to appreciate how difficult it is for a historian to achieve the impartiality which thankfully characterizes so many books produced today. These and many other works on the subject, including the justly famous biographies of the leading figures of Reformation days by Professor Pollard, will be found on library shelves, where there will also be journals containing articles which comment on developments locally as well as nationally. A good bibliography which will help you separate the wheat from the chaff is Mortimer Levine, *Tudor England* (Cambridge University Press, 1968), while books published between 1945 and 1969 are examined in G. R. Elton, *Modern Historians on British History, 1485–1945* (Methuen, 1970). Larger public and university libraries will have copies of J. S. Brewer and James Gairdner's treasured gift to historians of the Tudor period, *Letters and Papers, Foreign and Domestic, of the Reign of Henry VIII*. As you read the extracts and summaries of documents contained in that vast work, the source book for dozens of books written and yet to be written, the great characters of the period will, if you have any imagination at all, come to life, and you will understand them far better than you will by reading a twentieth-century biography.

Research is going on all the time, and new ideas are constantly being formulated. There are historians who will disagree with much of what has been written in this book, and doubtless many of the opinions and indeed facts quoted here will be disputed and disproved as new information comes to light. Many questions remain unanswered, and much research still remains to be done. Only now is Cranmer's diocesan register the subject of a thesis for a higher degree. Similar sources remain virtually unexplored in diocesan record offices up and down the country; while at parochial level, churchwardens' accounts, though often transcribed and sometimes printed, are still in need of scholarly analysis. Many hours of intellectual stimulation and the joy of discovery await anyone who decides to become a student of the English Reformation.

Appendix

GLOSSARY OF ECCLESIASTICAL TERMS USED IN THE TEXT

absolution: an ecclesiastical declaration of forgiveness of sins.

acolyte: a member of the highest of the minor orders of the Church's ministry, a candle bearer.

antiphoner: a book containing the choral section of services.

benefice: an ecclesiastical office with an income attached, usually a rectory or vicarage.

Blessed Sacrament: the consecrated bread and wine of the Mass or Communion Service.

bull: a written edict from the Pope.

canon of the Mass: that part of the Mass containing the prayer for the consecration of the bread and wine.

cardinal: one of the princes of the Roman Church, responsible for electing the Pope.

chalice: the cup containing the wine in the Eucharist.

chancel: the area of a church east of the nave, containing the main altar and choir.

chrism: a mixture of olive oil and balsam used for annointing in the sacraments of Baptism, Confirmation and Ordination.

Comfortable Words: in the Holy Communion service of the Church of England, passages from Scripture assuring the faithful that their sins will be forgiven.

Confirmation: a rite whereby the grace of the Holy Spirit is said to be conveyed in a new and fuller form to those who have received it in Baptism.

consecration: the setting apart of a thing or person for Divine service: in the Mass, the act whereby the bread and wine become the Body and Blood of Christ.

convent: a religious community of men or women.

cope: a semicircular cloak, often elaborately embroidered, worn by the clergy in church services, especially in procession.

Creed: a brief formal statement of Christian belief; in the Mass, the Nicene Creed.

cujus regio, ejus religio: 'In a (prince's) country, the (prince's) religion': the formula adopted at the Religious Peace of Augsburg (1555) by which the princes of the Holy Roman Empire were permitted to decide the religion of their own lands.

Curia: the Papal court.

deacon: a member of the third order of the Sacred Ministry; in Protestant Churches, usually an officer attending to the congregation's secular affairs.

De Heretico Comburendo: an Act of 1401, directed at the Lollards, providing for the burning of heretics.

dignitary: a person holding high ecclesiastical office.

dispensation: a licence granted by ecclesiastical authority to do something otherwise illegal under Canon Law, or for the remission of a penalty for performing such an act.

elder: in Calvinist churches, a layman assisting the minister in the administration and government of the church.

Epistle: the first lesson or reading at Mass, usually taken from the Epistles in the New Testament.

Eucharist: the Mass or Holy Communion.

exorcist: a person in minor orders, responsible for pouring out the water at Mass.

Gospel: the second lesson at Mass, taken from the Gospels in the New Testament.

Grace: the supernatural assistance of God, bestowed upon a recipient with a view to his sanctification.

heresy: the formal denial or doubt of any defined doctrine of the Catholic Faith.

heretic: one who commits heresy.

Holy Office: the congregation or court responsible for conducting the Inquisition.

Host: a sacrificial victim, and therefore the consecrated bread in the Eucharist, regarded as the Sacrifice of the Body and Blood of Christ.

Humble Access, Prayer of: a prayer in the Anglican Communion service in which the priest says how unworthy the communicants are to gather round the Lord's Table; it immediately precedes the Consecration.

incumbent: the holder of a parochial living.

Inquisition: the judicial persecution of heretics by special church courts; in Spain, very much under state control.

Justification by Faith: the doctrine that men achieve salvation solely by faith, and not by good works or personal merit.

lector: reader, one of the minor orders of the ministry.

legate *a latere:* a personal representative of the Pope, deputed for important missions of a temporary character.

legatus natus: the holder of a certain office which conveyed a legatine status *ex-officio*, e.g. the Archbishop of Canterbury.

Litany: a form of prayer consisting of a series of petitions or biddings which are sung or said by a minister, and to which the people make fixed responses.

liturgy: the prescribed services of the Church, sometimes specifically the Eucharist.

living: a benefice (q.v.).

mendicant friar: a member of one of those orders forbidden to own property in common, and therefore working or begging for a living.

missal: book containing the order of the Mass.

nave: the part of the church west of the chancel, assigned to the laity.

ordinary: one having immediate or *ex-officio* and not deputed jurisdiction, e.g. the archbishop in his province, the bishop in his diocese.

ostiary: a member of the lowest of the minor orders, with similar functions
    to those of a verger.
Papal Nuncio: a permanent diplomatic representative of the Holy See
    accredited to a civil government, and often of ambassadorial rank.
Paraphrases: a commentary on the Gospels written by Erasmus.
paten: the dish on which the bread is placed at Mass.
Pater Noster: the Lord's Prayer.
pontifical: the liturgical book containing the prayers and ceremonies for
    rites restricted to the bishop, e.g. confirmation, ordination,
    consecrating of churches, etc.
praemunire: the breach of statutes of that name designed to protect rights
    claimed by the English Crown against encroachment by the papacy.
Protestantism: the system of Christian Faith and practice based on the
    acceptance of the principles of the Reformation. The term is derived
    from the Protest of the reforming members of the Diet of Spires (1529)
    against the decisions of the Catholic majority.
province: an area under an Archbishop's authority, consisting of a number
    of dioceses.
Provisors, Statutes of: four laws passed in England in the fourteenth
    century to prevent the practice of Papal Provision or nomination to
    vacant benefices over the head of the normal patron.
prymer: a devotional book for the laity.
pyx: a receptacle designed to contain the Host.
religious: a member of an order of monks or nuns.
religious house: a monastery or nunnery.
rubrics: ritual or ceremonial directions at the beginning of service books or
    in the course of the text.
sacrament: a religious ceremony regarded as an outward and visible sign of
    an inward and spiritual grace.
schism: the division of a Church into two Churches, or the secession of part
    of a Church owing to difference of opinion on doctrine or discipline.
simony: the purchase or sale of offices in the Church.
solifidianism: Justification by Faith alone (*sola fides*).
stipend: a clergyman's official income.
surplace: a liturgical vestment of white linen with wide sleeves, worn in
    choir.
thurible: a metal vessel for the ceremonial burning of incense.
Unitarian: one who does not believe in the doctrine of the Trinity or the
    divinity of Christ, but that God is one person only.
usury: the exacting of interest on loans, forbidden by the Old Testament
    and the Councils of the Church.

Index

HISTORIANS MENTIONED IN THE TEXT